Spiritual Religion: A Study Of The Relation Of Facts To Faith. Being The Thirty-first Fernley Lecture Delivered In Newcastle-on Tyne, August, 1901...

John Greenwood Tasker

Spiritual Religion

A STUDY OF THE
RELATION OF FACTS TO FAITH

BEING THE THIRTY-FIRST FERNLEY LECTURE

DELIVERED IN NEWCASTLE-ON-TYNE, AUGUST, 1901

BY

JOHN G. TASKER

TUTOR IN BIBLICAL LITERATURE AND EXEGESIS
HANDSWORTH COLLEGE

London
CHARLES H. KELLY
2, CASTLE ST., CITY RD., AND 26, PATERNOSTER ROW, E.C.
1901

TO THE

REV. W. T. DAVISON, M.A., D.D.

PRESIDENT OF THE CONFERENCE

OF 1901

WITH GRATITUDE AND ESTEEM

Ye have purified your souls in your obedience to the truth.—
1 PET. i. 22 (R.V.).

To love truth for truth's sake is the principal part of human
perfection in this world and the seed-plot of all other virtues.
                                                    —JOHN LOCKÉ.

Magna est veritas et *prævalet*.—3 ESDRAS iv. 41.

CONTENTS

Chapter the First

Chapter the Second

THE SPIRITUAL NATURE OF MAN

v

Chapter the Third

GOD : A PERSONAL SPIRIT

Chapter the Fourth

COMMUNION BETWEEN GOD AND MAN

Chapter the Fifth

THE REVELATION OF GOD IN NATURE

Chapter the Sixth

THE REVELATION OF GOD IN HISTORY

Chapter the Seventh

ACCESS TO GOD THROUGH CHRIST

Chapter the Eighth

ACCESS TO GOD IN THE SPIRIT

Chapter the Ninth

COMMUNION WITH GOD IN THE CHURCH

The Church—a spiritual house :
  The conditions of its upbuilding ;
  The relation of the individual to the community.
Spiritual Religion endangered
  By the interposition of the Church between the soul and
    Christ,
  By the undervaluing of Church ordinances,
  By believers' neglect of their priestly duties and privileges.
The Fellowship of the Church :
  Personal Experience—
    Its value as evidence ;
    Its relation to the authority of Scripture.
  The testimony of the Christian community :
    A seal to the truth of God's promises ;
    A safeguard against personal delusions.
  The service of the Christian brotherhood :
    Spiritual acts of priesthood.

Chapter the Tenth

COMMUNION WITH GOD IN THE WORLD

That they may know the mystery of God, even Christ, in whom are all the treasures of wisdom and knowledge hidden.—Col. ii. 2, 3 (R.V.).

O Thou who, as our knowledge grows,
  In the world's later days,
The more Thou seem'st to clear the sky,
  The more dost hide Thy face:

As Science forging day by day
  Her close-link'd chain, withdraws
The once-felt touches of Thy hand
  For dumb organic laws:

The wider vision Thou hast given
  Yet is not wholly gain;
The truer vision scathes our sight;
  We cannot see Thee plain.

Enlarge our hearts and purge our eyes
  To bear Thy nearer light;
The world's young ignorance is o'er;
  Make us to know Thee right.

—FRANCIS TURNER PALGRAVE.

SPIRITUAL RELIGION

Chapter the First

INTRODUCTORY

The darkness is passing away, and the true light already shineth.
—1 JOHN ii. 8 (R.V.).

Help Thy vain worlds to bear Thy light.
—TENNYSON, *In Memoriam.*

EPOCHS of thought are not bounded by the lines which divide the centuries, and yet when the centuries are seen in historic perspective it is possible to distinguish their more prominent features and to define with sufficient accuracy their ruling ideas. The *Spirit of the Age* is not a meaningless expression, although it may elude the most skilful attempts to confine it wholly within the limits of any single formula. From the literature, and especially from the poetry and philosophy of an era, it is not difficult to determine whether its ideals were predominantly rationalistic, materialistic, or spiritual; such epithets do not mislead unless they are applied with mechanical rigidity.

The student of English literature, who passes from Thomson's *Seasons* (1730) or Pope's *Essay on Man* (1733) to the *Lyrical Ballads* (1798) of Coleridge and Wordsworth, has not crossed the frontier which separates two centuries, but he has entered a new zone of philosophic thought. He breathes the mental atmosphere of the nineteenth century, although he is reading words which were written in the last decade of the eighteenth ; the air is purer, the sky is clearer, and the horizon more extended : in short, he is conscious of a change of psychological climate. But such transitions are never abrupt, and in this instance the writings of Cowper and Burns occupy an intermediate position between Pope and Wordsworth. Hence, although " Return to Nature " is with truth said to be the dominant note in early nineteenth - century poetry, that new note had already been struck in *The Task* (1785) and *The Mountain Daisy* (1786).

Our generation has listened to singers in whose writings the progress of nineteenth-century thought from a materialist to a spiritual philosophy may be plainly traced, and there is no reason to doubt that their audience will be even more numerous in the twentieth century than during their own lifetime. If " Nature " was the dominant note in English poetry at the beginning of the nineteenth century, " Spirit " was the dominant note at its close. Matthew Arnold, Tennyson, and Robert Browning hold the foremost place amongst the poets of the Victorian age, who " in divers tones " and with characteristic variations have worked out the great twofold theme : Man the crowning glory of God's universe, and spirit the crowning glory of man. Browning, to whom Christianity powerfully appealed because it is a spiritual religion embodying spiritual ideals, describes in his last poem (1889) his vision of the reward which awaits " the adventurous quest " of those who " aspired from worst to best, *sought the soul's world*, spurned the worms'." To them

> Life is to wake not sleep,
>   Rise and not rest, to press
> From earth's level where blindly creep
>   Things perfected, more or less,
> To the heaven's height fair and steep;
>
> I have faith such end shall be:
>   From the first, Power was—I knew.
> Life has made clear to me
>   That, strive but for closer view,
> Love were as plain to see.[1]

The twentieth century will bring to ripe fruitage seeds of truth which future historians will discover in the writings of poets and philosophers, scientists and theologians, whose life-work or whose best work is already done. To trace the direction of lines of thought which at the same angle of inclination run on into the new century is, therefore, to pursue an inquiry fraught with practical interest to all who realise how great is the power which ideas exert on the lives of men and on the destinies of nations. In the beginning of the nineteenth century, when the German nation was prostrate before Napoleon, the voice that roused the people to a high sense of duty was the voice of the elder Fichte, the great idealist, whom his English biographer and translator, Dr. William Smith, describes as combining " the penetration of a philosopher with the fire of a prophet and the thunder of an orator." The basis of Fichte's famous *Addresses to the German Nation* is found in the leading ideas of his *Characteristics of the Present Age* (1806). In this work he who preached the " religion of a happy right-doing " asks : " What has been the highest and ultimate task of

---

[1] *Reverie.*

philosophy, but thoroughly to explore and vindicate the profound depths of the Christian doctrine?" He also maintains that "the whole character of the age is nothing else than its ascertained standpoint in respect of religion," and that "the principles from which the public religion of an age proceeds are to be found in the scientific and particularly in the philosophical character of *the preceding age.*"[1]

Never have the profound depths of the Christian doctrine been more thoroughly explored than in the latter half of the nineteenth century. The questions, therefore, which force themselves upon every thoughtful observer of the signs of the times are : *what principles underlie the scientific and philosophical progress of the period which must now be spoken of as the preceding age ? and how do the principles thus discerned affect the prospects of spiritual religion in the coming age ?* The outlook, we believe, is full of hope ; "the dawn is bright" say many wise watchers of the sky, for with thankful joy they saw the sun of the nineteenth century set behind clouds which were rosy with promise for the coming day. They cannot say "the darkness is past," nor could the apostle who had heard the message, "God is light, and in Him is no darkness at all" (1 John i. 5) ; but with St. John they rejoice to know that "the darkness *is passing away*, and the true light already shineth." At the midnight hour of the last day of the last century one of our younger poets heard "the voice of the Lord" saying :

> "I will make Me a city
> With room in your streets *for the soul*; "

[1] *The Characteristics of the Present Age*, pp. 226, 240.

and after describing the fair vision of the future of which Science gives the promise, he adds the timely exhortation:

> Let them look to the inward things, to the searchings of spirit,
> And cease from boastings and noise,

as becometh men who have heard the Voice:

> "Lo! I am the burster of bonds and the breaker of barriers—
> I am He that shall free," saith the Lord.
> "For the lingering battle, the contest of ages is ending,
> And Victory followeth Me." [1]

With the clear perception which is the reward of earnest philosophical study, Dr. Royce of Harvard University thus describes the last three centuries: the seventeenth century was *the century of Naturalism*; "the deification of Nature was surely the beginning of modern wisdom, an insight that whatever God is, He is not far from every one of us." In the eighteenth century men's doubts drove them from the study of Nature to *the study of Man*, "first of human reason, then of human conscience, then of all the human heart and soul." The chief characteristic of the nineteenth century was the exposition of *the evolutionary theory of Creation*; and "surely if the great Spirit is anywhere to be manifest to us, then it should be in the growth of humanity. . . . For our nineteenth century it is just the change, the flow, the growth of things that is the most interesting feature of the universe." [2] Hence, although it is difficult to characterise the intellectual life of any era as a unity, it is impossible to deny that " after Darwin " marks an epoch in religious as well as scientific thought. Theological problems are now discussed in phraseo-

---

[1] Stephen Phillips, *Midnight—31st December*, 1900.
The Spirit of Modern Philosophy, p. 273 f.

logy which is borrowed from the philosophy of Evolution, and the inevitable result is that very subtly but very powerfully language reacts upon thought. Religion will gain by the process, if without loss of sterling value its well worn terminology is re-issued as current coin bearing the impress of present truth. The passing of a century which has chiefly studied "the growth of things" forces upon us the inquiry: Has the progress no aim, or is it the evolution of a spiritual purpose?

To reply at once that there are unmistakable evidences of *a spiritualistic trend in modern thought* is not to prejudge the issue; for eminent scientists acknowledge that it is becoming more and more difficult to exclude conceptions of the spiritual from attempts to explain the natural. " In to-day already walks to-morrow," and the probability is that in the early years of the twentieth century the study of Psychology will prove as attractive and absorbing as during the nineteenth century the study of Biology has been. *From spirit to nature* is the true order, for in the search for knowledge priority is determined by the degree of certainty. To begin with " matter," when Science can tell us so little of the constitution of its ultimate atoms, is to reverse that order, and to run the risk of interpreting facts belonging to a higher sphere by terms which have been defined by induction from facts belonging to a lower sphere. On the other hand, to begin with the Self of which man's knowledge is most immediate and certain is to secure a point of vantage from which to study our fellow-men and the problems of Sociology; and to begin with Spirit and its manifestations in human life is to secure a point of vantage from which to study nature and the enigmas of the material universe.

The facts of the religious consciousness *cannot be isolated from other facts*; a thorough analysis of spiritual experience brings us at some stage or other into contact with every sphere of human knowledge. Doubtless the fundamental truths of the Christian religion are thereby exposed to attack from many different quarters; but on the other hand, the failure of faith's numerous foes to refute its main presuppositions becomes strong presumptive evidence that those presuppositions hold good. They are no true friends of faith who sever religious knowledge from all other kinds of knowledge; in so doing they secure a temporary peace by withdrawal from the field of conflict. Every refusal to face facts is a present defeat, and the continuance of such tactics cannot but result in complete disaster. On two conditions the ultimate victory of faith depends: the clear statement of the facts of spiritual experience, and the frank recognition of the facts revealed by science. He is a fellow-worker with the truth who destroys any of the perishable elements in the foundation upon which faith rests; but he is also a fellow-worker with the truth who unmasks the fictions which have been mistaken for facts by the enemies of faith. A friendly yet discriminating critic of the Ritschlian theology has done well to point out that in biblical exegesis the interests of truth have been promoted not by the adoption of peculiar methods of study, but by the application to Holy Scripture of scientific principles of interpretation. Researches into Church history have also become more fruitful as they have been pursued in close connexion with investigations in profane history, and as the results in one department have influenced the conclusions arrived at in the other.

"Why, then, should the only sphere of knowledge over which is written *noli me tangere* to warn off all philosophers be the knowledge of the truths of religion? Is not this the very domain to which every investigator ought to have a free pass securing admission?"[1]

Faith and Science cannot be relegated to spheres which never touch. If faith rests on facts, these facts furnish a legitimate domain for scientific investigation; and if science asserts that any of these facts are fictions, the grounds on which the assertion is based must be examined without prejudice. Faith has nothing to lose but everything to gain from unbiassed study of the facts of the religious consciousness and from impartial inquiry into the historic evidence for the facts which constitute God's revelation of Himself to man. The gain is not always immediately manifest, and may sometimes look like loss; but seeming loss is gain, if it serve to show that "the things that are shaken" and that can be removed have been wrongly identified with "the kingdom that cannot be shaken" (Heb. xii. 27 f.). For example, the seeming loss which results from giving up the ancient estimate of the scientific value of the biblical story of Creation will prove great gain, if earnest seekers after truth are no longer blinded to the spiritual glory of the narrative because, like Huxley, they have been taught that the Pentateuchal cosmogony is divine truth.[2] During the nineteenth century theology and science have often been in conflict: sometimes the attempt to undermine faith has failed, because philosophic fictions have been mistaken for scientific facts; but sometimes theology has

[1] Wendland, *Albrecht Ritschl und seine Schüler*, p. 31.
[2] *Life of Huxley*, vol. i. p. 167.

been driven from positions rendered untenable by the destruction of fortresses long regarded as strong defences of the faith. The Church has too often forgotten that the weapons of her warfare are spiritual; therefore her soldiers have been "baffled to fight better"; but retreat is not defeat, and withdrawal from outposts which ought never to have been held may be the condition upon which the final victory depends.

In this Lecture an attempt will be made to estimate the influence upon spiritual religion of modern modes of thought, the main object of our inquiry being to show *the relation of facts to faith.* For such a study the Christian consciousness will furnish the view-point, or—to use an illustration suggested by a German phrase [1]—the point which we fix as our *Orient,* and from which we take our bearings. By observation of the sun or of the stars the mariner discovers his latitude and longitude; then he can fix his own whereabouts and the relative position of the port he hopes to gain or the quicksands he desires to avoid. To find our whereabouts in the strange seas into which the currents of modern thought have carried us, it is necessary to fix the Orient; then in confidence we may voyage farther. If in our hearts the Day-star has arisen (2 Pet. i. 19), that bright dawn of grace has taught us once for all how to mark the East and how to determine whether we are sailing westward to the "golden harbour," or are drifting towards "seas of death and sunless gulfs of doubt." Spiritual religion implies an inward experience so real that to the spiritual man it becomes a standard by which in his investi-

[1] *Orient*irungspunkt.

gations he *tests* (ἀνακρίνει) all things.[1] (Cp. 1 Cor. ii. 15, R.V. margin.)

It is hoped that ambiguities which still cleave to the word *Religion* may be avoided by the addition of the word *spiritual*. That some such qualifying epithet is needful was made manifest in the course of a discussion in the *Times* on "The Decay of Experimental Religion." Sir Edward R. Russell ascribed to the influence of the Church Revival "a great change in religion at its very base so far as the individual is concerned," and, after describing the religious man of fifty years ago, declared that "it is now possible to be a religious man at far less expenditure of mind, with much less—and perhaps no—spiritual experience." In one of the replies to this letter, "Caritas" spoke disparagingly of emotional religion, and maintained that in High Church manuals "personal religion, meditation, prayer, self-surrender to God, are taught with fervour and with insistence quite as great as the fervour of the early Evangelicals."[2] Spiritual religion includes both the experimental religion of the one writer and the personal religion of the other. Much of the prejudice against what is called "emotional religion" may be traced to a confusion between the popular use of the word "heart" for the seat of the emotions and

---

[1] The objection that the spiritual man *imagines* this inward experience to be real rests, as will hereafter be shown, upon the unwarranted assumption that what is subjective is imaginary or unauthorised. But subjective truth is "that which is true because the individual has learnt aright to apprehend and see a truth, whose reality is *not dependent on himself*. What is real in and to my mind is therefore subjective to me. It is subjectively that the objective is realised."—Moberly, *Atonement and Personality*, p. 142.

[2] See *Times*, November 9 and 12, 1898.

its biblical use for the seat of man's personal life. The love of the heart is not a sentimental affection, it is the love of conscious resolve ; and heart-religion is not an excitement of the feelings, but an experience which affects the whole personality—emotions and intellect, conscience and will. It follows that the appeal to Christian experience is an appeal to facts and not to feelings,—an appeal to facts which are not only manifest to the inward consciousness, but also manifest in the outward life, and of which, therefore, others may take knowledge (cp. Acts iii. 10). Between spiritual religion and orthodoxy, and between spiritual religion and sacramentarianism, it ought not to be necessary to discriminate ; the high function of the sacraments is to promote spiritual religion, and the great task of Theology in one of its departments is to furnish a reasoned explanation of the facts of the Christian consciousness.

Spiritual religion is εὐσέβεια, *pietas*, the "godliness" of the New Testament as distinguished from θρησκεία, *cultus exterior*, the "religion" of which St. James writes : "Pure religion and undefiled before our God and Father is this, To visit the fatherless and widows in their affliction, and to keep himself unspotted from the world" (Jas. i. 27). When this passage is quoted in depreciation of heart-religion, it is misunderstood ; it gives no support to those who minimise the inward and spiritual aspects of religion, nor to those who so exalt its outward aspects as practically to identify it with morality and works of benevolence. The purpose of St. James is to assert the supremacy of Christianity as contrasted with Judaism, even when the two religions are compared only in their *external* aspects. Christianity is a spiritual religion, and its outward expression is not in acts of ritual, but in deeds of kindness.

Herrmann thinks that Christians are fully agreed as to *the meaning of personal Christianity*: " It is a communion of the soul with the living God through the mediation of Christ. Herein is really included all that belongs to the characteristic life of Christendom—revelation and faith, conversion and the comfort of forgiveness, the joy of faith, and the service of love, life with God alone and life in Christian fellowship. All this is then only truly Christian when it is experienced as communion with the living God through the mediation of Christ." [1] Without at this stage discussing what Herrmann means by " the mediation of Christ," we may heartily concur in his statement that personal Christianity as thus defined " can arise in spite of wrong teaching, and can remain alive amid obsolete ecclesiastical forms." He and other writers of his school would be surprised to learn that such expressions breathe the very spirit which animated John Wesley. When theological controversies are conducted on this assumption, the strife of words will provoke neither bitterness nor wrath. A hopeful sign of the times is the growing disposition to recognise that Christians may have much to learn from teachers whose creed is incomplete, but whose writings reveal the reality of their inner life of faith. To his Roman Catholic critics Harnack says: " That the end to which our striving is directed is the same—the seeking, finding, and keeping hold of God—may be confidently granted on both sides." [2] Our response may be made in the words of Wesley in his

[1] Herrmann, *The Communion of the Christian with God*, p. 7.
[2] *History of Dogma*, vol. vi. p. 108.

Sermon on a Catholic Spirit: "Though we cannot think alike, may we not love alike? May we not be of one heart, though we are not of one opinion? Without all doubt, we may."[1]

In the course of this inquiry it will therefore be taken for granted that Christians of various schools of thought would accept such a simple, albeit comprehensive definition of religion as Dr. John Caird's: "*Religion is the communion of the soul with God.*" He who has this direct and heartfelt experience of God[2] is a religious man, though access to God may have been found by a different path from that which led others into His presence. He who enjoys this communion with God "has light within his own clear breast, and sits i' th' centre," from which point of vantage alone it is possible to see how lines of evidence which start from opposite points of the compass and seem to move in contrary directions do really converge; in his religious consciousness he finds a standard by which to test the sufficiency of every " view of the world " (*Weltanschauung*), ancient or modern, agnostic or theistic :

> That (is) his test for every thought—
> Will it lift us up nearer to God or not?[3]

Harnack, in his latest work, finds the essence of the Christian religion to be "something supernatural, a gift from above, not a product of ordinary life. . . . It is a purely religious blessing, the inner link with the living God "; in his view the most characteristic feature of the Christianity of the Apostolic Age is " that individual Christians, moved

---

[1] Sermon xxxix. § 4. [2] Cp. Pascal's phrase, *Dieu sensible au cœur.*
[3] W. C. Smith, *Poems.*

by the Spirit of God, are placed in a living and entirely
personal relation to God Himself"; the author of the Acts
of the Apostles is "conscious that the Christian religion
would not be the highest and the ultimate religion unless
it brought every individual into an immediate and living
connexion with God."[1] The question, therefore, is: *How
does man attain to this consciousness of personal communion
with God ?* The majority of those who possess it are content
to believe that Christianity must be true, because it satisfies
the deepest needs of man's moral and religious nature ;
a genuine spiritual experience enables them to banish,
if not to silence disquieting thoughts. The memorable
words of Professor Tyndall furnish those who maintain
this attitude with a scientific warrant: "Religious feeling
is as much a verity as any part of human consciousness,
and against it on its subjective side the waves of science
beat in vain." But in these days of mental unrest many
are perplexed by "head-doubts" who are free from "heart-
doubts." The joy of the Lord is their strength, and enables
them to "cleave ever to the sunnier side of doubt, and cling
to faith"; but their faith would have greater assurance
and their testimony would gain an accent of deeper conviction, if they could dismiss from their minds the haunting
fear that they are shutting their eyes to new light. If
in this Lecture the writer has been able to focus on the
pathway of any such believer some rays of light which
have helped to scatter his own unbelief, his main object
is attained ; but his joy will abound if any seeker after
God should learn that the gloomy shadows which
have attended his quest vanish with fuller knowledge, and

[1] *What is Christianity?* pp. 62, 164 f.

that in truth " the clouds themselves are children of the Sun."

Spiritual religion, as already defined, implies *facts concerning man and concerning God.* Christianity is an historical religion as well as a religion of experience, and facts of history as well as facts of experience may be scientifically examined. Faith awaits the results of such investigations without fear, confident that in the future as in the past Science by removing intellectual hindrances to belief will make manifest its true foundations. The experience which is the result of faith is itself a fact, the significance of which Science cannot afford to overlook ; nor dare Faith be blind to any fact which scientific research may bring to light. In studying the relation of facts to faith, the following course of thought will be pursued. The facts which physiology and psychology reveal as to the constitution of human nature, and the distinction between facts and assumptions in materialistic interpretations of the universe, will be considered in Chapters II. and III. from the point of view of the Christian consciousness ; evidence will therein be adduced of a distinct reaction in favour of the reasonableness of belief in the two chief presuppositions of spiritual religion : that *man is made in the likeness of God,* who is spirit ; and that *God is the Father of spirits,* and can commune with His children. In Chapter IV. the possibility of *communion between God and man* will be illustrated by analogies drawn from the facts of our own experience as we strive to reveal ourselves to our friends. Chapters V. and VI. will deal respectively with the *Revelation of God in Nature and in History,* with the view of ascertaining to what extent the teachings of natural religion are based on facts, as well as of estimating the importance of facts which point in the direction of faith, though of necessity they fall short of demonstrating its presuppositions. In Chapters VII. and VIII. facts of history and of experience will be examined in the light of Scripture and of the Christian consciousness, the special purpose of the inquiry being to discover in what sense the early Christians understood the teaching of the Apostles that *man's access to God is through Christ and in the Holy Spirit*. Chapters IX. and X. will aim at showing, by an appeal to Church history and to Christian experience, that *communion with God* is a privilege realised not only in solitary fellowship, nor only *in the Church* with the aid of its manifold ministries, but also *in the World* by faithful fulfilment of the duties of our daily calling and by cheerful discharge of our obligations to serve our fellow-men. In social work as well as in Church fellowship the Christian has hours of blessing, when

> He feels he cannot die,
> And knows himself no vision to himself,
> Nor the high God a vision.[1]

What is involved in this knowledge of Self and in this vision of God we must now consider.

[1] Tennyson, *The Holy Grail.*

Chapter the Second

THE SPIRITUAL NATURE OF MAN

Though our outward man is decaying, yet our inward man is being renewed (ἀνακαινοῦται) day by day.—2 COR. iv. 16.

> Let us be like a bird, one instant lighted
> Upon a twig that swings;
> He feels it yield, but sings on unaffrighted,
> Knowing he hath his wings.—VICTOR HUGO.

SPIRITUAL religion implies, as the Bible always assumes, that *the essential element in human nature is spirit*. The question that concerns us, therefore, is not, "Has man a soul?" but, "Is man, who cannot forget that he has a body, —is man a spiritual being?" There are moments when in the divine presence man finds it impossible to doubt the reality of his spiritual nature, for this postulate of faith is verified in every act of communion with God. Even in the ages before Christ, when the conception of self-conscious personality, as common to God and man, was but dimly apprehended, the language of the Hebrew psalmists expresses their consciousness of spiritual fellowship with such vigour and vividness as to suggest that, although they had no clear knowledge of a future life, they could not conceive of fellowship so intimate being interrupted by death (cp. Pss. xvi. 11, xvii. 15). But there are also moments when man hears the " dull, one-sided voice " daring

2

to affirm—what is " at best a vague suspicion of the breast "
—that man's life is nothing but a weary pilgrimage

> From that first nothing ere his birth
> To that last nothing under earth ! [1]

When, therefore, materialistic science loudly asserts that
spirit has been banished from the universe, our first duty
is to ask the " masters of those who know" on what facts
this claim is based, and then we may inquire whether
science or philosophy has any reasonable explanation to
offer of the facts of the religious consciousness.

During the latter half of the nineteenth century the
old question, *What is man ?* has been thrust into the fore-
front of the battle of the philosophies, in consequence of
the researches and speculations of Darwin, Huxley, and
Herbert Spencer. The first effect of the publication of
Darwin's *Origin of Species* (1859) was to give a materialistic impulse to philosophic thought, but before the end
of the century spirit had once more asserted its claims,
and the result of a more thorough study of the " self " which
is presupposed in all sensation and knowledge and volition
is a widespread conviction, outside the ranks of professed
theologians, that the materialistic explanations of the facts
of consciousness are untenable.

So recently as 1885, however, a careful observer of the
tendencies of modern thought, who was quick to distinguish between the main current and the surface eddies,
wrote : " It is the belief that the soul can commune with
God, can make itself heard by Him, can hear His word

[1] Tennyson, *The Two Voices.*

and obey it, can feel His love and return it, which is so out of keeping with the physical science of the day, and so subversive of scientific maxims and exhortations." [1] Mr. Hutton would probably have modified this judgment had he been writing to-day, for he would have perceived the importance of the distinction, which is becoming more generally recognised, between the actual results of scientific research and the inferences which philosophy draws from the facts. The belief that man is a spiritual being, capable of knowing and loving God, is "subversive" of no truth which Science has demonstrated, but only of certain "maxims" which are really philosophical hypotheses whose claim to rest upon a scientific induction from facts may prove on investigation not to be well founded.

During the early years of this century the forces of Materialism will, it is said, lead the attack upon all spiritual beliefs. It is well, therefore, to remember that with Science, when properly understood, Theology can have no quarrel. It is not with Materialism as a science, but with Materialism as a philosophy, that Theology comes into conflict. Theology is the philosophy of spiritual religion, and Materialism is one of several philosophies of Nature, human nature being included. Both theology and philosophy may need to modify their conclusions and to revise their hypotheses in the light of the facts which such sciences as Physiology and Psychology bring to light. But neither in philosophy nor in theology can any theory claim acceptance, unless it is consistent with all the facts, and unless it interprets the whole content of human experience as recorded in history and as verified by ourselves and others to-day.

[1] R. H. Hutton, *Aspects of Religious and Scientific Thought*, p. 335.

From the Science of Psychology most light may be hoped for on the constitution of human nature, but before asking the psychologist for his interpretation of the facts of experience it is necessary to show that no recent advances in physiology have rendered his investigations superfluous. In view of persistent attempts to explain mind as the ultimate product of matter, and to identify mental and physical processes, the question must be asked: "*Can physiology account for the facts of man's mental life?*" With the noteworthy exception of Haeckel and his disciples, who repeat the oft-refuted dogmas of Materialism, the utterances of modern physiologists are increasingly in harmony with the spiritual conception of human nature. There are many who recognise the impossibility of resolving thought into a physiological function, and there are few who would say with Cabanis that "the brain secretes thought as the liver secretes bile," or with Jakob Moleschott that "thought is a motion of matter."

Modern physiologists are unwilling to express an opinion, when the facts which come within the spheres of their own investigation do not warrant a positive conclusion. The most acute observer of the molecular changes which take place in the brain during a mental process never discovers either that matter in motion is a sensation or that a brain change is a change of purpose. Neither the movements nor the secretions of the material organism can constitute a thought or an emotion. Volition and sensation are as incomprehensible now as they were before Sir Charles Beale's memorable discovery of the motor and sensitive columns in the spinal cord with the corresponding nerves of motion and sensation. The knowledge of the media by which sensations are transmitted to the seat of consciousness accounts for " the ringing of the bells at the receiving-station of the brain," but it does not account either for the reception of the message and the comprehension of its significance or for the dispatch of the answer and the resultant action. In brief, it yields no proof of the materialistic assumption that thought is the product of physical energy.

Professor Huxley, who expressed his agreement with Dr. Tyndall's statement that " the chasm between physical processes and the facts of consciousness is intellectually impassable," argued that we are quite as ignorant, " when the motion of one billiard-ball is imparted to another," of the connexion between these two successive physical changes, as we are when one of the two is mental. But when motion produces motion it is a case of transference, not of transformation ; in the two successive physical changes, scientists trace a constant *quantitative* relation between the vanishing cause and the effect which takes its place, whereas thought stands in no such relation to its physical antecedents, and remains wholly unaccounted for. Mental facts are " faults " in the series of physical phenomena, for " the law which forbids the transference of physical energy into anything but physical energy places *the facts of consciousness outside the chain of physical sequences.*" [1] But thoughts and feelings are none the less facts of which our knowledge is immediate and certain, though Physiology can discover no physical evidence of their existence.

Reference has been made to the law of the *Conservation of Energy* by whose aid Science has gained so many of its

[1] Herbert, *Modern Realism Examined*, p. 29 f.

triumphs. This law is a generalisation from observed facts, and has been verified by the accuracy of scientific predictions based upon it; it asserts that the total amount of physical energy in the universe can neither be diminished nor increased, although it may change its form, as, *e.g.*, when motion produces heat or heat produces motion. By some modern writers this law is so interpreted as to involve acceptance of the materialistic theory of mind. In a popular work which claims to be a simplified statement of the teachings of Darwin and Spencer, we are told that " if the phenomena of mind are not capable of like mechanical explanation as the phenomena of stars and planets and of vegetable and animal life, Evolution remains only a speculation to fascinate the curious. If there be anything done by man which lies outside the range of causation, then the doctrine of the Conservation of Energy falls to pieces, for man has the power to add to that which the physicist demonstrates can neither be increased nor lessened. . . . The story of Creation is shown to be the unbroken record of the evolution of gas into genius." [1]

It is important to remember, as Höffding points out, that " the discoverers of the law of the conservation of energy *started from entirely spiritualistic premisses.*" Mayer, who formulated its fundamental axiom, " several times pronounced himself opposed to materialism, and expressed his conviction that scientific truths are related to the Christian religion as streams and rivers to the ocean." The Englishman Joule, and the Danish physicist Colding, arrived at the same result by different paths, but they agreed in holding Theistic views of Creation. Colding

[1] Clodd, *Plain Account of Evolution.*

says : " The thought that natural forces are imperishable first occurred to me in connexion with the view that the forces of nature are akin to the spiritual element in nature, to the eternal reason as well as to the human mind. In other words, I was led to the idea of the constancy of natural forces by a religious conception of life." [1] Moreover, the inconsistency of the materialistic argument, as usually stated, is manifest, for whilst assuming that states of consciousness are effects of physical antecedents, it denies that thoughts can give rise to movements. From this dilemma there seems to be no way of escape open to the materialist : either it is false to assume that sensations and thoughts are caused by nervous changes, or it is impossible to deny that mind has influence in the material sphere. The same amount of physical energy is expended by the commander of an army whether he says " Halt !" or " Charge !" but the destinies of nations may be changed by the mental decision, which determines the action of his soldiers.

This law of the Conservation of Energy was considered in its relation to *the origin of consciousness* by a celebrated German physiologist, Du Bois-Reymond, at a Conference of scientists and physicians held at Leipzig in 1872. His statements have an important bearing upon Natural Theology, and their significance is enhanced by the fact that Du Bois-Reymond pursued his studies in the avowed hope that physical science might succeed in tracing all changes in the material world to the movements of atoms. Hence in this instance the materialistic hypothesis " received its severest blows from one who was most desirous that the mechanical theory should be found to be universally

[1] *History of Modern Philosophy*, vol. ii. p. 497.

true, and who was, notwithstanding, sorrowfully obliged
to admit its inadequacy in certain specific cases." Having
shown that the mechanical theory of the universe cannot
account for the origin of mind, Du Bois-Reymond proceeds
to examine intellectual processes, and concludes that they
cannot be explained by their material conditions. To quote
his own words, which are the result of patient examination of mental phenomena : " Motion can only produce
motion, or transform itself into potential energy. Potential
energy can only produce motion, maintain statical equi-
librium, push or pull. The sum-total of energy remains
constantly the same. More or less than is determined by this
law cannot happen in the material universe ; the mechanical cause expends itself entirely in mechanical operations.
Thus the *intellectual occurrences* which accompany the
material occurrences in the brain *are without an adequate
cause* as contemplated by our understanding. They stand
outside the law of causality, and therefore are as incomprehensible as a *mobile perpetuum* (perpetual motion) would be."

Physical Science, as represented by this accomplished
specialist, confesses her inability to explain such fundamental facts of consciousness as " I feel pain," or " I hear
music," or " I exist." Physiology cannot deny that Tennyson was expressing a true and profound philosophy when
he said, " You never, never can convince me that the ' I '
is not an eternal reality, and that the spiritual is not the
true and real part of me." [1] With the poet agrees Professor
Fiske, whose philosophical writings have done much to
prove that the theory of Evolution is not inconsistent with
the spiritual view of human nature : " The correlation

[1] Tennyson, *A Memoir*, vol. ii. p. 90.

of Forces exhibits Mind as in nowise the product of Matter, but as something in its growth and manifestation outside the parallel. It is incompatible with the theory that the relation of the human soul to the body is like that of music to the harp; but it is quite compatible with the time-honoured theory of the human soul as indwelling in the body and escaping from it at death."

At the close of the nineteenth century Professor Ernst Haeckel restated his materialistic solution of the riddle of the universe. His work is an example of what Lange in his *History of Materialism* deplores: it is one of the "books of popular science which base themselves upon materialistic views as calmly as if the matters had been settled long ago." There is no possibility of misunderstanding Haeckel's words; in his view "human nature which exalted itself into an image of God . . . has no more value for the universe at large than the ant, the fly of a summer's day, the microscopic infusorium, or the smallest bacillus. Humanity is but a transitory phase of the evolution of an eternal substance, a particular phenomenal form of matter and energy."[1] But Haeckel does not answer the objections of scientists who dispute his interpretation of the facts of human consciousness. No light is cast upon the problem by arguments which disprove what none but a materialist would think of advancing; as, *e.g.*, that if the soul were a gaseous substance, it would condense under high pressure at a low temperature. Moreover, it is illogical to write as though the impossibility of collecting the *fluidum animæ immortale* in a flask made

[1] *The Riddle of the Universe*, p. 249.

one whit more plausible the theory that the soul is a function
of the brain.   It is a mere evasion of the questions at issue
to say that " senile decay in the brain and other organs"
accounts for the change of view to which more mature
thought led such men as Du Bois-Reymond, Virchow,
and Wundt,—scientists who found that the hypotheses
of materialism were insufficient, when they pushed their
researches into regions whither Haeckel declines to follow
them. Haeckel's references to Kant are reduced to an
absurdity by Dr. Braasch of Jena : " The 'young, severely
critical Kant' (*N.B.* he was fifty-seven years old) was
convinced that the *Pure Reason* alone cannot defend the
three great buttresses of Mysticism—God, Freedom, and
Immortality.   The 'older *dogmatic* Kant' (*N.B.* he was
sixty-five years old, which is about Haeckel's present age)
discovered that 'these three great hallucinations' were
postulates of the *Practical Reason*." [1]   Thus Kant's famous
argument from the direct commands of the moral law
to the existence of God is dismissed without refutation,
because the great philosopher was eight years older when
he published it than when he wrote the work whose negative conclusions are approved.   But Haeckel's plea that he
has been a consistent advocate of Materialistic dogmas
throughout his life does not absolve him from the charge
of ignoring successful attacks upon the materialistic creed.

The majority of modern scientists do not, like Haeckel,
deny the spiritual nature of man ; many decline to express
any opinion, but some bring forward positive and weighty
evidence which is distinctly adverse to the inferences of
materialists. Last year the Professor of Physiology in

[1] *Ueber Ernst Haeckel's Welträthsel*, p. 18.

the University of Glasgow published a remarkable address, in which he says : " The thoughtful physiologist runs no risk of becoming a materialist in the grosser sense of the term. The study of his science amplifies and enlarges his views of matter ; but when his analysis is pushed to its extreme limits he is brought face to face with another order of facts and another order of phenomena. These we call spiritual, although we cannot define what we mean by this word any more than we can define what we mean by matter or energy." [1]

So far as the attitude of physiologists is concerned, it may be confidently affirmed that the new century opens with the prospect of a better understanding between Science and Theology. But the same statement may be made with equal emphasis in regard to *the attitude of psychologists* ; their interpretations of the phenomena of man's mental and moral life often rise to lucid expositions of a lofty philosophical faith. It is significant of much that the close of the nineteenth century should witness the publication of the great work of one of our most profound thinkers—Dr. Ward's *Naturalism and Agnosticism,*—for in it the manifold problems suggested by these two words are studied from the point of view of psychology. The author's brilliant article on " Psychology " in the *Encyclopædia Britannica* established his claim to speak on this subject with the authority of an expert, and his new work is another proof that the more scientific is the Psychology, the more impossible does it become to ignore the soul (*psyche*) and to reduce psychology to physiology. Professor

[1] M'Kendrick, *Science and Faith,* p. 62.

Drummond, whose sensitive mind was susceptible to every change of thought that affected the spiritual life, truly says: "To many men of science, judging by the small estimate in which they hold philosophy, the day of mental science apparently is past. To an enlightened theology it is the science of the future."[1]

Another question, therefore, must now be asked: "*What do psychologists teach in regard to the spiritual nature of man?*" Have they not striven to explain the "Self" as a delusion, and to deny its permanence by identifying it with the fleeting series of its feelings? Less than fifty years ago agnostic philosophers were endeavouring to dissolve personality into a mere series of conscious states; but scientific thinkers of the present day pronounce the attempt a failure, and repudiate the assertion that modern psychology leads to a materialistic philosophy. Mr. Titchener, who is an enthusiastic advocate of the method of experimental introspection as used by Professor Wundt in his psychological laboratory at Leipzic, says: "It is often asserted, on the one hand, that modern psychology leads to a materialistic metaphysics, and on the other, that it proceeds in flagrant disregard of the modern theory of knowledge. I cannot admit that either charge is well founded. I believe that materialism — the Ontology of *Kraft and Stoff* and of the *Belfast Address*—is wholly unpalatable to scientific thinkers of the present day, and that the chief danger which besets the psychologist, in particular, is that of falling not into a crass materialism, but into an equally crude spiritualism."[2]

Deeper search into the mystery of "Self" has proved how

[1] *The New Evangelicalism*, p. 17.   [2] *Primer of Psychology*, p. viii.

irrational it is to describe as " a pure fiction " the one reality that man knows. One need not be a philosopher to perceive that the principles of all sound reasoning are violated whenever an attempt is made to deny the existence of that which the denial must assume in order to be valid. " The one thing which *anyone knows* as mind," says Mr. Herbert Spencer, " is the series of his own states of consciousness." This is virtually, though not formally, a negative statement which denies the existence of a permanent Self, and yet implicitly reaffirms it. Else how can there be " anyone " to " know " that the mind is only a series of conscious states ? He who doubts the existence of Self must assume it, for is it not the Self that doubts ? " A feeling exists only because there is a subject that feels it. A thought exists only because there is a thinker. . . . Self is the necessary background of thought. . . . The self-conscious subject is called Spirit, Person, Soul, Mind, Self, Ego, Intelligence. It is the 'I' of individual experience." It is unnecessary to multiply quotations from eminent psychologists, for as Mr. D'Arcy adds : " It may be doubted if many remain who would profess a purely materialistic creed."[1] Augustine's words, though fifteen hundred years old, are not antiquated ; they are true to the facts of consciousness : " As for me, the most certain of all things is that I exist. Even if thou deniest that I am, and sayest that I deceive myself in this, thou confessest that I am ; for if I do not exist, I cannot deceive myself."[2]

Modern psychology accepts the Cartesian maxim, *Cogito, ergo sum*, but interprets it not as an argumentative, but as an explicative statement. " I think, therefore I

---

[1] *Short Study of Ethics*, ch. i. §§ 3, 10.
[2] Quoted by Höffding, *History of Modern Philosophy*, vol. i. p. 154.

am " means " I think, that is to say, I am." There is no
begging of the question, but a simple affirmation that
known thought is impossible, unless someone knows it, so
that he who knows that he thinks knows that he exists.
Professor James of Harvard, one of the most distinguished
of living psychologists, has given clear expression to the
truth, which is essential to spiritual religion : that *experience cannot be limited to mere perceptions of the senses.*
In his fine analysis of experience he shows that the followers
of Hume " ignore the phenomena of attention and seldom
use the word "; and yet who can deny that as the power of
volition is dependent upon our possession of the power of
attention, " the question whether attention involve the
principle of spiritual activity . . . is the pivotal question of
metaphysics, the very hinge on which our picture of the
world shall swing from materialism towards spiritualism,—
or else the other way." Professor James, for ethical reasons,
maintains that *voluntary attention is a spiritual force,*
and points out that " the reasoning which denies that
attention involves spiritual activity is not science but materialistic speculation." To say that " the consciousness does
not count," and therefore does not exist for science, is as
" intensely reckless " as to use arguments from analogies
drawn from rivers and other " material phenomena where
no consciousness appears to exist," and to extend them
" to cases where consciousness seems the phenomenon's
essential feature." If Mr. Spencer were right in regarding
" the creature as absolutely passive clay, upon which experience rains down," then " dogs bred for generations in
the Vatican " ought to become " connoisseurs of sculpture,"
whereas " an eternity of experience of the statues would leave

the dog as inartistic as he was at first, for the lack of *an original interest* upon which to knit his discriminations." [1]

This argument is valid in a yet higher sphere. Man knows himself to be a spiritual being by his consciousness of *an original interest in the spiritual world*; hence it is intensely reckless to say that the religious consciousness does not count. Psychology may, however, explain why our spiritual perceptions are so often vague and indistinct. Interest in the phenomena of the spiritual world may become dulled; the intensity and range of spiritual experience will always depend upon our *attention* to the spiritual realities which appeal for recognition to the eyes of the heart (Eph. i. 18, R.V.). "My experience," says Professor James, "is what I attend to." In the spiritual philosophy of Tennyson this absolute conviction of the reality and activity of the Self finds frequent expression. Self is revealed not only in thought and affection, but pre-eminently in every act of moral choice.

> Live thou! and of the grain and husk, the grape
> And ivy berry, *choose*; and still depart
> From death to death thro' life and life, and find
> Nearer and ever nearer Him, who wrought
> Not matter, nor the finite-infinite,
> But this main miracle, that thou are thou,
> With power on thine own act and on the world. [2]

Free-will is rightly regarded as the very "nerve of personality." Probably the most important contribution in recent years to the understanding of this vexed question will be found in the philosophical works of Professor T. H. Green. [3]

---

[1] *Principles of Psychology*, vol. i. ch. xi.   [2] *De Profundis.*
[3] See *Prolegomena to Ethics*, bk. ii. ch. i.; and cp. Davison, *The Christian Conscience*, p. 66 ff.

When " motive " is accurately defined and distinguished from " desire," a conflict of motives is impossible ; *the will is free because it is determined by motive,* for the " Self " determines which desire shall prevail and become the motive to action. The importance of this distinction is obvious. The deeper needs of human nature must remain unsatisfied unless man has the power to resist the desire which at the moment is most urgent. In every act of man there is not only the consciousness of the presence of a motive, but also the consciousness of the adoption by the Self of an impulse ; without this acceptance of the desire it cannot be transformed into the motive which determines action.

> Who speaks of man, then, must not sever
> Man's very elements from man,
> Saying, " But all is God's "—whose plan
> Was to create man and then leave him
> Able, his own word saith, to grieve him,
> But able to glorify him too
> As a mere machine could never do.[1]

This brief description of personality may help some of its readers to *appeal to their own moral consciousness,* and so to gain or to strengthen the conviction : " I, too, can think and know that *I* am thinking ; I, too, can act and know that *I* am acting." A true conception and a vivid realisation of our own personality will reveal to us " abysmal depths " which our plummets cannot sound, but it will help our thoughts to rise to a worthier conception of God, the perfect Personality. There is the most intimate connexion between the two halves of Browning's profound saying :

> He at least believed in soul
> And was very sure of God.[2]

---

[1] Robert Browning, *Christmas Eve,* v.   [2] *La Saisiaz.*

Let a man examine himself as he pays attention to phenomena which appeal to his intelligence, as he responds by some deliberate act of choice, and he will discover that the permanent self is not a delusion; let him further observe how in intercourse with his friends he gains fuller knowledge of himself, and the conviction will be deepened within him that he is not incapable of yet more complete spiritual development in fellowship with God.

There are few who can say with Jean Paul Richter, "Never shall I forget when I stood by the birth of my own self-consciousness. . . . On a certain forenoon, I stood a very young child, within the house door, and was looking out toward the door-pile, as in an instant the inner revelation 'I am I,' like lightning from heaven flashed before me; in that moment I had seen myself as I, for the first time and for ever." Very few boys or girls—like Mansel, a future Bampton Lecturer, in his childhood—have been overheard to say, "My hand, my foot, but *what is me?*" Nevertheless, in the development of self-consciousness there comes a moment when the child makes the discovery, "I am not what I see, and other than the things I touch"; in after-years he may be unable to remember how he learnt "the use of I and me," but henceforth he can *isolate himself* from "the frame that binds him in." At each stage in our subsequent inquiry this elementary psychological truth must be borne in mind: *every advance in the knowledge of "Self" is gained in intercourse with some "Not-Self."* The enriching of personality is conditional upon the extension of the sphere of interests. A man may live for self or for his family, for the town in which he is a citizen or for his fatherland, for his fellow-men or for his God.

3

These are alternatives in which the higher does not exclude the lower ; but if the narrower sphere is chosen, the penalty is the impoverishing of self. Probably it is impossible to live an absolutely self-centred 'life ; but the suggestive expression should warn us that the lessening of the circumference of our interests involves the shrinkage of the Self. "Personality in the individual is the capacity for society, fellowship, communion. The δύναμις of κοινωνία."[1] This helpful definition is taken from an able philosophical study written to expound the truth that no capacity of our personal life reaches its goal except in communion with others. In the interests of spiritual religion it is all-important to remember that personality is developed not only by the Altruism which lives for others, but also by the Altruism which lives for God, and not merely for self or for humanity. Our self-consciousness being awake, we learn in human fellowship gradually to know ourselves ; and when " our consciousness eternal wakes," we learn in converse with God to know our higher Self ; as that divine fellowship becomes more intimate and is more constantly realised in the communion of saints and in the service of man, the spiritual nature attains its highest development and our souls grow in the knowledge of God.

> Take all in a word : the truth in God's breast
> Lies trace for trace upon ours impressed ;
> Though He is so bright and we are so dim,
> We are made in His image to witness Him.[2]

---

[1] Richmond, *An Essay on Personality as a Philosophical Principle*, p. 21.
[2] Robert Browning, *Christmas Eve*, xvii. Cp. also Henry More's profound saying : " *Nullus in microcosmo spiritus, nullus in macrocosmo Deus.*"

Chapter the Third

GOD: A PERSONAL SPIRIT

God is spirit: and they that worship Him must worship in spirit and truth.—JOHN iv. 24 (R.V. margin).

> Because God lives, I live; because
> He thinks, I also think;
> I am dependent on no laws,
> But on Himself, and without pause;
> Between us hangs no link.
> —DR. GEORGE MACDONALD.

SPIRITUAL religion implies *the personality of God*. Only with a God who is spirit can man who is spirit hold communion. "A need, a trust, a yearning after God" is our spirit's "lode-star," and progress in the spiritual life depends upon "looking towards that star." Before Neptune was discovered, the size and position of the planet, whose existence was only a hypothesis, were accurately described by astronomers from observation of the disturbances in the motion of Uranus. The best explanation of our heart's restlessness is that our finite spirits are attracted by the Infinite Spirit, "unseen but felt,"—attracted to Him from whose presence so often we fain would flee. The spirit of man, until it knows the peace which comes from God's forgiveness, is "like the troubled sea; for it *cannot* rest" (Isa. lvii. 20, R.V.); the prophet's fine simile reminds us that the soul's restlessness

is in itself a proof of its nobility, for the alternating ebb
and flow of its desires is the evidence of its susceptibility
to heavenly influences as well as to the drawings of earth.
" Man stands," says Lamennais, " with one foot in the finite
and the other in the Infinite, and is torn asunder not by
four horses, but by two worlds." Job knew that " the
Almighty" was troubling him, even when he cried, " Oh
that I knew where I might find Him" (Job xxiii. 3, 16);
and before our hearts find rest in God, knowledge of ourselves may teach us that only " the Father of spirits " can
satisfy the longings of the children who bear His likeness.
The God whom our spirits crave is neither the impersonal
God of the Pantheist nor the remote God of the Deist. To
seek the Pantheist's God is unnecessary, and to seek the
Deist's God is useless. Our Lord said, " My Father worketh
even until now, and I work" (John v. 17, R.V.),—simple but
profound words, which prove that to His consciousness God
was neither impersonal nor inactive. The " Father of our
Lord Jesus Christ" is a God with whom His children can
commune.

The God of the Pantheist and the God of the Deist are
alike in this : *both lack the power of self-revelation.* But
a being unable to reveal himself is powerless to draw forth
personal reverence and love ; hence there can be no communion with Divinities who lack this all-important element
of personality. Ritschl's words apply to modern as well
as to ancient systems of thought, when he says of the speculations of Greek philosophers, " They failed to satisfy the
essential conditions of the religious view of the world, partly
in so far as they surrendered the personality of the Godhead
thus identified with the ground of the world, partly because

they had to give up the active influence of a personal God upon the world."[1]

The word "personality" when applied to God must mean at least all that it means when used of man. To say this is not to incur the condemnation, "Thou thoughtest that I was altogether such an one as thyself" (Ps. l. 21), nor to claim that, in learning what man is, we "find out the Almighty unto perfection" (Job xi. 7); it is simply to affirm that if man is "the image and glory of God" (1 Cor. xi. 7), *Will, Intelligence, and Love* will be manifest in the divine personality *in infinite perfection.* "Betwixt beings absolutely unlike there can be no communion"; spiritual religion is beyond our reach, unless "God's nature is essentially one with ours, and what we call thought, intelligence, mind is in essence the same in God and in us . . . in Him the infinite thought or reason, in us that of beings to whom the inspiration of the Almighty hath given understanding."[2]

The assertion of this *essential likeness* between God and man does not, however, involve the denial of that "*transcendent difference*" which Mr. Herbert Spencer holds to be all-important.[3] These two conceptions are not mutually exclusive, as Dr. Ward has demonstrated in his masterly criticism of Spencer's doctrine of "The Unknowable"; if they were contradictory ideas, and we were shut up to absolute difference, it would be vain to exhort men to seek after God. "But if we may attribute to that Unknowable even Causality or Power, then so far we assimilate it to our-

---

[1] *Justification and Reconciliation*, p. 208.
[2] Dr. John Caird, *University Sermons*, p. 28.
[3] See *First Principles*, p. 109.

selves, as being causal agents; and were it not that such is our nature, we could not find that such, too, in transcendent measure is the nature of God." [1]

In modern philosophic thought the conception of God as *more than personal* has acquired importance. But some who call the Absolute " super-personal " are as anxious to avoid the " mistake " of affirming personality, as they are averse to the errors involved in speaking of God as impersonal. Such a use of the word *super*-personal tends to confusion of thought; unless personality can be affirmed without reservation, it is misleading to employ a word which means personal *and more*. The difficulties presented to our minds by the conception of God as an Infinite Personality are not lessened by any such expedient; the seeming contradiction between the two expressions is not removed until with Lotze we perceive that " only the Infinite is completely personal."

To speak of the Infinite Spirit as the only complete personality is to give full expression to the truth which philosophers have striven to put into words by saying that God is personal and more than personal. The distinction between *individuality and personality* must first of all be clearly recognised. An individual is a distinct, circumscribed existence; he is defined by those qualities which separate him from the other members of his class. But the individuals from whom he differs are persons like himself, the essential elements of personality being those qualities which he possesses in common with the rest. If this be not the true conception of personality, communion between

[1] *Materialism and Agnosticism*, vol. ii. p. 269.

man and man as well as between man and God is inconceivable; nevertheless, it does not follow that human personality is the measure of divine personality. The growth of our own minds, as the varied though limited experiences of life enrich us, helps us to conceive of a mind whose experiences are not limited by time—a mind to whose development, therefore, no bounds can be fixed. Such a conception of a mind which is Infinite because its experiences are infinite enables us to attach a real though doubtless inadequate meaning to the expression " Infinite Personality." At this point, moreover, the Christian doctrine of the Trinity, whilst contradicting no truth of reason, comes to our aid and makes known the truth to which reason could never have attained. In personal affection man is conscious of relation to another person ; hence the revelation of an eternal distinction of persons in the Godhead interprets the revelation that " God is love." Theology completes and harmonizes the highest teachings of philosophy when it affirms that " God is personal and also super-personal, that in Him there is a transcendent unity which can embrace personal multiplicity." [1]

This conception of God as a personal spirit, to whom we may ascribe Will, Intelligence, and Love, is regarded by many influential writers as incompatible with the teachings of modern Science. *The principle of Causality* has been so interpreted as to be inconsistent with the thought of a personal *Will* operative in Nature ; *the theory of natural selection* has been so expounded as to render personal *Intelligence* superfluous ; and *the struggle for existence* has been

[1] D'Arcy, *Idealism and Christianity*, p. 94.

supposed so to multiply the proofs of Nature's cruelty as to banish *Love* from the cosmic process.

With characteristic lucidity and force Professor Huxley stated the scientific objection to the thought of a Personal Will operative in Nature, when, in his *Lay Sermons*, he declared that the progress of Science "means the extension of the province of what we call matter and causation, and the concomitant gradual banishment from all regions of human thought of what we call spirit and spontaneity." This objection, however, rests upon *a mechanical interpretation of the principle of Causality* : if the universe be a machine subject only to natural (*i.e.* mechanical) laws which are uniform in their operation, then it is manifest that in such a universe there can be no room for the energy of a Personal Will. But the mechanical theory breaks down when it attempts to account for all the facts ; as, *e.g.*, it cannot explain how the machine was started. Du Bois-Reymond—whose impartiality as a witness is established by the fact that he looks forward to the time when more perfect knowledge will have solved the problem of the Origin of Life—declares that "the problem of the origin of Motion is insoluble." [1]

No light is cast upon this problem by Haeckel's assumption that movement is an innate and original property of substance. The third of the "important conclusions" which he draws from the discoveries of modern astronomers and physicists is that "substance is everywhere and always in uninterrupted movement and transformation ; nowhere

[1] *The Seven Riddles of the Universe.* See Kennedy, *Natural Theology and Modern Thought*, p. 52.

is there perfect repose and rigidity."[1] The world-enigma which the origin of motion has presented to the profoundest thinkers is evaded by the unverifiable hypothesis that universal movement is the supreme law of substance— a hypothesis which Haeckel himself contradicts when he speaks of substance in its "original state of *quiescence*." But this is only one of the many hypotheses to the invention of which at the end of the nineteenth century this famous scientist is driven when, leaving the sphere of investigation for which he is eminently qualified, he attempts to prove that the universe is its own creator.

Given infinite substance endowed with the primitive property of feeling; *given* that the world, including Man, is made of this original substance, which feels pleasure in condensation and pain in expansion; *given* that matter and ether thus evolve themselves out of substance; *given* that matter and ether, which fill the universe and leave no empty space for spiritual beings, possess feeling and will "naturally in the lowest degree"; *given* that the primeval atoms have only to arrange themselves in various groupings and in varying numbers in order to form an acid, a metal, or a thought-producing brain-cell; *given* that in the course of ages, infinite substance in perpetual self-originated motion produced of itself sun, moon, and stars, and that "our mother earth was formed of part of the gyrating solar system"; *given* a period of time variously estimated at fifty millions or fourteen hundred millions of years, but sufficiently long for the earth to become cool and for water to form itself on its surface so that living organisms may survive; *given* that protoplasm endowed

[1] *The Riddle of the Universe*, p. 248; cp. p. 223.

with life is a purely natural product ; — *given* that this long but by no means exhaustive list of Haeckel's assumptions is a string of facts, yet it remains as inexplicable as before how without the direction of an Intelligent Will there could emerge out of the chaos a world of order and of beauty and the human personality which is worth more than all the world.

The controversy to which the publication of Haeckel's work has given rise in Germany is full of significance. Scientists as well as theologians have protested *in the name of exact science* against his materialistic view of the world. Indeed, the utterances of representative thinkers afford encouraging proof that, on the one hand, Science recognises the necessity of including in her investigations all the facts, and the invalidity of her conclusions outside her proper sphere ; whilst, on the other hand, Theology is willing to welcome Science as an ally, to give due weight to every fact brought to light by her researches, and to study with open mind every new revelation of God's methods of working in the world. Historical critics like Hilgenfeld and Loofs do not pronounce Haeckel's attack upon Christianity a failure because his conclusions clash with the dogmas of the faith, but because he accepts fables as facts and uses arguments which have become obsolete by the discrediting of his authorities.[1] Scientists like Reinke and Baumann, philosophers like Troeltsch and Paulsen, do not say that Haeckel has failed to solve the riddle of the universe because his findings are inconsistent with their respective theories, but because his position is rendered untenable by reason of his own inconsistencies and indifference to facts.

[1] See Loofs' pamphlet, *Anti-Haeckel*.

Reinke, the famous botanist, does not find it so easy as Haeckel to believe that living protoplasm is a natural product. On the contrary, living protoplasm is such an extraordinarily difficult and peculiar chemical combination, and modern chemists with all the resources that science now places at their disposal find it so impossible to produce it, that Reinke refuses to ascribe to blind accident what is so utterly beyond the reach of human skill directed by reason. Speaking as a naturalist and with no theological bias, he declares it to be as incredible that the result of purely accidental combinations of material atoms should be a living cell, as that the shaking of a sack of letters should produce a poem; therefore he is driven to the conclusion that the origin of life cannot be explained save by a creative act of God. Moreover, Reinke, still writing as a naturalist accustomed to watch the evolution of organic life, affirms that the marvellous process is inexplicable unless the operation of the law of causation is directed by *an invisible architect* endowed with intelligence and purpose. The scientist, who traces the evolution of the germ-cells of plants into the perfect forms which exactly represent their respective types, but who cannot discern any evidence of Intelligence at the heart of the cosmos, is compared to the man who, standing before an oil-painting, has no eyes for the idea which finds artistic expression in the picture, but only for the canvas and the colours. The facts which viewed from one side appear as " dominant impulses " in organisms, viewed from another side appear as the manifestations of an intelligent purpose which guides the organic processes to their predestined goal.[1]

[1] *Die Welt als That*, p. 304 f. See Braasch, *Ueber Haeckel's Welträthsel*, p. 24 ff.

The riddle of the universe is complicated by the existence of beings who know that within limits they can execute the designs which they have themselves conceived. The introduction of this new element into the problem requires that its solution shall account not only for the existence of organisms which unintelligent Force could never have produced, but also for the existence of *self-conscious beings who are themselves producers of thought and sources of causal energy.* Hence the arguments already employed to refute the materialistic explanations of inorganic and organic life apply with increased cogency to the mental life of man. Scientists allow that the principle of Causality is violated by the application to the phenomena of thought and will of a theory of Causation which is based upon observation of the phenomena of the material universe.

Man's inability to explain how the mental act of volition can affect the motor nerves is no proof of his incapacity to influence the forces of nature by the decisions of his will. So long as Science keeps within her proper sphere as defined by such modern thinkers as Kirchhoff of Berlin and Mach of Vienna—that is to say, so long as Science is content to describe and not to explain the course of nature—the facts to which the human consciousness bears witness cannot be ignored. When, therefore, self-consciousness is scientifically analysed and the psychologist affirms that the same facts, which to the physiologist appear as molecular motion in the brain, are known to him as concentration of attention or change of purpose, it cannot be unreasonable to believe that the phenomena of the natural world may be correctly viewed by the scientist, and yet may present quite another aspect to the divine mind. So long as Physiology, which knows nothing of Personality, does not claim to present an exhaustive interpretation of human nature, its findings are quite consistent with a Psychology which recognises Personality. And so long as Natural Science, which knows nothing of Divine Personality, does not claim to present an exhaustive interpretation of Nature, its findings are quite consistent with a Theistic philosophy which recognises Divine Personality.

> We who believe Life's bases rest
> Beyond the probe of chemic test,
> Still, like our fathers, feel Thee near.[1]

It would, however, be idle to deny that the teachings of modern Science on *The Uniformity of Nature* proved a hindrance to faith, until the revival of ancient teaching on the immanence of God in nature altered the aspect of the problem. The regular sequence of events in the natural world now becomes an evidence that He " with whom there is no variableness" forsakes not the work of His hands.

> My heart is awed within me, when I think
> Of the great miracle that still goes on
> In silence round me, the perpetual work
> Of Thy creation, finished, yet renewed
> For ever.[2]

Moreover, the progress of Science has led to the use of the phrase *The Unity of Nature* as a more correct description of the universe. " Uniformity may be merely mechanical, but Unity is essentially a spiritual conception . . . we cannot conceive a merely material unity, since spirit is the only unifying agent that we know." Hence, by those who hold that this unity rests in God, the laws of Nature are regarded

[1] Lowell, *Ode for the 4th of July*, 1876.   [2] Bryant, *Forest Hymn.*

as the regular methods employed by God in the execution of His vast and beneficent designs; miracles are therefore not antecedently improbable, for " if nature is sustained only by its intimate union with spirit, it is no wonder that the processes of nature should be modified for an adequate spiritual end." [1]

After a thorough and candid inquiry into the many complex problems involved, Dr. Ward says: " Nature points to one supreme Intelligence as its only sufficient reason by the regularity and completeness of its mechanism, and to one prime cause by the inertness of all the parts of that mechanism. Neither Naturalism nor Agnosticism can render this reasoning obsolete." [2] Nor can this argument be weakened by any necessary inference from the facts upon which the theory of Evolution is based. The argument from Design, which Darwin rejected, has been strengthened by the researches of his disciples. Evolutionists delight to expound the marvels of *the new teleology*, and maintain that their teaching is not consistent with the conception of the universe as a machine, but quite consistent with the conception of an ever-present God of whose working Nature is the true revelation. " The process of Evolution is itself the working out of a mighty teleology, of which our finite understandings can fathom but the scantiest rudiments." [3]

The Darwinian biology has restored man to the place of honour and dignity from which the Copernican astronomy

[1] Illingworth, *Personality, Human and Divine*, pp. 103, 106.
[2] *Naturalism and Agnosticism*, vol. ii. p. 257.
[3] Fiske, *Cosmic Philosophy*, vol. ii. p. 406.

seemed to have dethroned him; for if his home is not the centre of the physical universe, he himself is Creation's crown and goal. *" Evolution culminates in mind "* is the witness of Physiology: a comparison of the human body with the bodies of animals immediately below man in the scale of existence proves that it " is not an advance only as regards brain and nervous system (as many suppose), but it is a more complicated machine in every detail of its structure." Careful and prolonged scrutiny of physiological phenomena has convinced scientists like Professor M'Kendrick that there is an orderly progression which culminates in the manifestation of mind; " this can only be accounted for by recognising thought as underlying, controlling, directing living phenomena. . . . And if thought underlies all vital phenomena, and so controls these as to secure as an ultimate phenomenon the manifestation of itself, then there can be no difficulty, from the point of view of Science, in believing in the existence of a Great Being, who is the Source of Energy of this universe and of all living things." [1]

These witnesses are quoted because their conclusions are the result of independent and unbiassed study of the facts presented to them in their respective spheres of scientific investigation. The value of their evidence cannot be discounted by any suggestion of prejudice in favour of faith; inasmuch, therefore, as their conclusions are quite consistent with a spiritual view of the universe, they tend to confirm our faith in God as a personal spirit. That the testimony adduced is a sign of the movement of *modern* thought appears from the words of Sir William Turner in his

[1] *Science and Faith,* p. 42 ff.

Presidential Address to the British Association, delivered in the closing year of the nineteenth century. The address dealt almost exclusively with scientific subjects, but its exposition of the evolutionary theory of creation is in complete harmony with the teaching of Theism in regard both to the origin of life and the origin of mind. " It is enough," says an agnostic critic, " to prompt the thought that the one immortal thing in the world is supernaturalism itself " ; and it is enough, the Theist may add, to warrant the hope that in the new century the relations between Theology and Science will be based on a clearer mutual understanding, and will result in richer mutual gain. " We know not," says Sir William Turner, " as regards time, when the fiat went forth, ' Let there be Life, and there was Life.' All we can say is that it must have been in the far distant past, at a period so remote from the present that the mind fails to grasp the duration of the interval. Prior to its genesis our earth consisted of barren rock and desolate ocean. When matter became endowed with life, with the capacity of self-maintenance and of resisting external disintegrating forces, the face of nature began to undergo a momentous change. Living organisms multiplied, the land became covered with vegetation. . . . At last man came into existence. His nerve-energy, in addition to regulating the processes in his economy which he possesses in common with animals, was endowed with higher powers." [1]

A difficult question still remains : Can belief in the Divine Personality be reconciled with the theory of Evolution, which maintains that *the struggle for existence* is a condition

[1] *Nature*, September 6, 1900, p. 448.

of progress? Love is an essential element of personality, and many who find in the world proofs of an intelligence that designs and a will that controls, ask in doubting anguish, " Is there any evidence that the purpose revealed in Nature is a purpose of Love ? " It may be that the final solution of this problem of pain is beyond our reach. Some, like Dr. A. R. Wallace, assert that the seeming tragedies of nature have been exaggerated, our imagination picturing them as more awful than they really are; for though we see with painful vividness the outward fact, we do not see the merciful anodyne. This is, doubtless, an alleviation of the difficulty, although it cannot be regarded as a complete explanation. Some, like Professor Drummond, find in nature the germs of Altruism as well as of Egoism, and maintain that alongside of the struggle for existence there is a struggle for the life of others. But love in the cell that divides in order that it may not die cannot be identified with the spiritual love that " lays down its life " for others. " Creation is due," says Dr. Fairbairn, " to the moral perfection of the Creator, who is so essentially Love that He could not but create a world that He might create Beatitude." [1] This fine thought may explain the existence of the world, but it does not follow that from study of the world *as we know it* we should be shut up to the conclusion that Love was the creative impulse.

Love is a relation between persons; not to Nature, therefore, must we look for a complete revelation of the divine Love. But if the doctrine of Evolution has rendered the idea of " an absentee God " inconceivable, in restoring God to the world it has made impossible the thought that He

[1] *Christ in Modern Theology*, p. 413.

is indifferent to the world's sorrows. Hence the reverent student of His works may catch glimpses of a purpose, long thwarted by sin and contingent on "the revealing of the sons of God" (Rom. viii. 19, R.V.)—a purpose which, when realised, shall include the hushing of Creation's groans, the ending of its long travail, and the restoring of the harmony to which it was predestined in Christ (Rom. viii. 22). It is "through Him" that God shall "reconcile all things unto Himself, having made peace through the blood of His cross; through Him, I say, whether things upon the earth, or things in the heavens" (Col. i. 20, R.V.). "Nature includes man as well as the brutes, and the merciful and moral man as well as the savage. And the Christian may say with all reverence that Nature includes, or rather is included by Christ, the Word of God by whom it was made. And the Word was made flesh to teach us that vicarious suffering, which we see to be the law of Nature, is a law of God. . . . It is precisely because the shadow of the Cross lies across the world that we can watch Nature at work with 'admiration, hope, and love,' instead of with horror and disgust."[1]

> There is in God, some say,
> A deep but dazzling darkness.[2]

---

[1] Inge, *Christianity and Mysticism* (Bampton Lecture, 1899), p. 314.
[2] Henry Vaughan.

Chapter the Fourth

COMMUNION BETWEEN GOD AND MAN

The Lord spake unto Moses face to face, as a man speaketh unto his friend.—Exod. xxxiii. 11.

All true growth in religion, whether in the past or the present, springs from the communion of man with the immediate loving God.
—Charles, *Doctrine of a Future Life*, p. 3.

THE purpose of the two preceding chapters has been attained, if it has been made clear that on *a priori* grounds neither science nor philosophy can deny the possibility of communion between God and man. Researches which extend the circle of light multiply the points of contact with the darkness; scientific progress reveals new mysteries, in presence of which philosophy either confesses the limitations of her knowledge or suggests theories which assume a final mystery. Such theories, it will always be found, approximate more and more closely to the mystery of God revealed in Christ, as they become more comprehensive in their grasp of truth, include a greater number of facts, and embody the results of more thorough investigations. When on strictly scientific grounds it is acknowledged that neither biology nor physiology can explain the mystery of man, and that neither mechanics nor physics can explain the mystery of the universe, it is both arbitrary and illogical to say that the testimony of the Christian consciousness to the reality of spiritual communion is delusive.

No attempt was made in the previous chapter to state, even in outline, the well known *arguments for the existence of God.* To Ritschl and his followers it may be readily granted that neither scientific nor philosophical interpretations of the world can yield the Christian conception of God; but that fact furnishes no valid reason for despising such knowledge as men have gained by exploring these lofty heights, nor for withholding our gratitude from those who would help us to find in such studies steps by which we too may ascend the Mount of Vision. Few deny that in man and in nature there is a spiritual element; some say sadly, "we shall never know"; many confess frankly that a purely mechanical view of the world increases its mysteries; and others find that scientific research and philosophical speculation are ways that lead to God. Such knowledge of God is not attained "by sudden flight"; "Let us know the Lord" means "let us *follow on* to know" Him; but to all seekers who are content patiently to follow on, the promise is fulfilled: "His going forth is sure as the morning" (Hos. vi. 3, R.V.). To them the world is no longer irrational, for on their path the Sun has risen, whose beams illumine all mysteries of thought, though into its depths man cannot gaze.

Self-knowledge is one of the paths that lead upwards to "the shining tablelands to which our God Himself is moon and sun"; the reason why many a prodigal is wandering on the dark mountains is that he has never "come to himself," and therefore has never said, "I will arise, and go to my Father." A modern Evolutionist, on whose feelings and conscience the Bible exercised no influence, and upon whom the " soft and gentle " figure of Christ never really laid hold, testifies that in study of himself he came to see that it is " impossible to expel spiritual mystery from the centre of our experience." [1] *Study of the facts of human consciousness* cannot, of course, bring to light all the facts of the religious consciousness, but it may remove objections and suggest helpful analogies. If Science leaves us open to the influences of Nature and of other minds, it leaves us open also to the influences of the divine Spirit. Dr. Crozier's inquiries into the spiritual experiences of his friend during a revival of religion convinced him that Science was powerless to explain them; and Mr. William Watson finds that in human life there are great emotions which have a higher origin than the senses :

> One not pale of blood, to human touch
> Not tardily responsive, yet may know
> A deeper transport and a mightier thrill
> Than comes of commerce with mortality.[2]

Such facts are not explained when a sensational philosophy describes them as transcendental and delusive, but they warrant the hope that the foundations of spiritual religion will be strengthened by the scientific study of such facts of spiritual experience as conviction and conversion.

Psychologists prove by their *analysis of consciousness* that experience is " not tantamount to the mere presence to the senses of an outward order " ; from such experience we could deduce neither the truth of number that one and

---

[1] Crozier, *Autobiography of an Evolutionist.*   [2] *Apologia.*

one are necessarily two, nor the direct command of the moral law to which conscience bears its witness. This demonstration of the fact that many kinds of natural agencies are required to explain our ordinary experience establishes the right of the religious consciousness to be heard when it bears witness to *the reality of experience for which no natural agency can account.* " How," asks Professor James, " could our notion that one and one are eternally and necessarily two ever maintain itself in a world where every time we add one drop of water to another we get not two but one again ? In a world where every time we add a drop to a crumb of quicklime we get a dozen or more ? Had it no better warrant than such experiences, at most we could then say that one and one are *usually* two." Again, " the moral principles which our mental structure engenders are quite as little explicable *in toto* by habitual experience having bred inner cohesions. Rightness is not *mere* usualness, wrongness not *mere* oddity, however numerous the facts which might be invoked to prove such identity." [1]

Thus the keenest analysis of personality fails to explain away as a delusion the Self which is the presupposition of all experience—the Self without whose activity even the fundamental principles of arithmetic are unintelligible, not to speak of metaphysical axioms and moral maxims. " *What we mean* by one plus one *is* two ; *we make* two out of it. We are masters of our meanings." The validity of this argument is not affected by adding inherited ancestral experiences to the experience of the individual. If it is impossible for some elements of our knowledge to have entered *any* mind by the " front door of the senses "; if

[1] *Principles of Psychology*, vol. ii. ch. xxviii.

our ordinary experience is inexplicable, unless there are other doors which admit " recondite " natural agencies, — then surely it cannot be deemed incredible that there are doors of the inner chamber which open heavenwards, and through which divine influences may enter to enrich the spiritual experience of man.

Communion is reciprocal : a personal spirit communicates with another personal spirit who responds. In the intimacy of true fellowship there is interchange of thought, mutual consciousness of the satisfaction of desires, glad yielding of the will to love's constraint. False conceptions of God may render such communion impossible, though false conceptions of man are perhaps more frequently a hindrance to the modern mind. Herrmann does well to contend earnestly that one may have an intellectual grasp of the idea of the Eternal without experiencing " the first awakening quiver of religion . . . for a Deity such as we might conceive by thinking solely of the idea of the Eternal would indeed impress men with a sense of His power and dignity ; but He would also hold us at a distance, and abandon us to the feeling of our utter insignificance, by showing us the vanity of all the affairs of human life." [1] These words are true of the Deist's God who lives his life apart from the world, yet has a personal life of his own ; but they state clearly an objection which applies with even greater force to every philosophy that reduces the idea of God to an intellectual abstraction. Worship " at the altar of the Unknown and the Unknowable " must be, as Professor Huxley perceived, " mostly of the silent sort."

[1] *Communion with God*, p. 49.

Spiritual communion with God is impossible if a mere law or power or tendency is the only Divinity we know. Of the law of gravitation Browning says :

> Ay, but man puts no mind into such power !
> He never thanks it, when an apple drops,
> Nor prays it spare his pate while underneath ; [1]

but his words apply to all philosophies and would - be theologies that substitute " It " for " Thou." Neither thanksgiving nor prayer can be offered to " It."

> Force and force,
> No end of forces ! Have they mind like man ?

The reason why no form of Pantheism can satisfy the soul that longs for God is that *personality in its full meaning is essential to both man and God*, if they are to hold spiritual communion. If the suppliant cannot say " Thou art " to the God to whom he prays, or if in saying " Thou art " he means less than when he says " I am," adoration, petition, and thanksgiving are alike impossible. " O Thou that hearest prayer, unto Thee shall all flesh come . . . O God of our salvation . . . Thou makest the outgoings of the morning and evening to rejoice " (Ps. lxv. 2, 5, 8). Difficult as it may be to grasp the whole truth of which the Deist and the Pantheist caught partial glimpses, nevertheless to lose sight of either aspect of it is to imperil spiritual religion. To think of God as the Creator of the world and as transcending all His works, but to forget that He is now upholding and directing all things, is to remove Him to a height beyond the reach of our spirit's soarings ; on the other hand, to think of God as immanent in nature

[1] *A Bean-stripe, also Apple-eating.*

and in man, but to forget that He is above all as well as in all, is to identify the human and the divine consciousness, to paralyse the powers of the soul, to weaken the pinions on which alone it can rise to God.

> Having God in thee,—a completer Soul,
> Be sure than thou alone!—thou not the less
> Complete in choice and individual life,
> Since that which sayeth *I* doth call Him, *Sire*.[1]

Our finite mind with its limited powers of perception may be unable to combine its separate visions of truth into one worthy conception of the perfect sphere of which transcendence and immanence are the two halves. But these two postulates of thought have rewarded seekers after God, who starting from different points have pursued the quest for truth in different directions; and they are verified in every real act of communion, whether it be the prayer that "fleets beyond this iron world and touches Him that made it," or the willing self-surrender which is the response of man to the seeking spirit of God. "As it is impossible," says Amiel, "to be outside God, the best is consciously to dwell in Him; . . . God is present in nature, but nature is not God; there is a nature in God, but it is not God Himself. I am neither for immanence nor for transcendence taken alone."

Philosophies that teach *the immanence of God* in all things cannot exclude the soul of man from the sphere in which divine energies are constantly at work, nor can they raise any objection to the Christian doctrine that "the Father of Spirits" influences human spirits in all ways in which one person may influence another. The

[1] Dr. George Macdonald.

danger of such philosophies lies in their vague statements in regard to the mutual relations of personal beings. If the consciousness of man is merely " a vehicle of the Eternal consciousness," the human personality is blended with the divine ; but communion is reciprocal, and implies that the one personal spirit is distinct from the other. The testimony of the religious consciousness is that divine influences neither dwarf nor destroy the personality in which man dwells alone ; on the contrary, the spirit of man is stimulated by the divine Spirit to higher forms of activity, and is enabled to realise its nobler powers. " Less of self and more of Thee " may be misunderstood both by the philosopher and by the mystic, for we shall not have more of God by becoming straitened in ourselves. Modern Idealism—the philosophy which has done so much to defend spiritual religion from the assaults of materialistic science—has not always avoided this extreme. " God is not a spirit beyond the stars, He is spirit in all spirits," must not be so interpreted as to suggest that the human spirit is only a mode of existence of the divine Spirit. Such teaching lessens the sense of human worth, and when carried to its logical issues contradicts the witness of conscience to man's personal responsibility.

" The way to God lies through the conscience," and no analysis of personality is complete which ignores its witness. Conscience not only recognises one action as wrong and another as right, but enforces the obligation," This I ought, and that I ought not to do " ; it also pronounces sentence of condemnation upon all who know that they have done the wrong or left the right undone. *Man's moral consciousness* is a fact that cannot be denied, except by assuming that all our knowledge of ourselves is untrustworthy. Kant demonstrated the impossibility of deriving the Imperative[1] of Duty from observation of nature where a different kind of necessity holds sway. " It would be absurd to say that anything in nature ought to be other than it is in the relations in which it stands. Indeed, the word *ought* when we consider the course of nature has neither application nor meaning." Nature may present to the will various and powerful impulses, but it is beyond their power to pronounce the word *ought*. The sense of obligation cannot be derived from the observation of nature ; still less can it originate of itself in the mind of man. Doubtless, it is the law of our being that reason should control the appetites and desires, but the authority of conscience is not explained by saying that a man is a law unto himself. When conscience utters the words " ought " and " must," man hears *the echo of a higher Voice* which claims his reverence and obedience. Moral consciousness means what Mr. R. H. Hutton has well described as " the quiver of the whole nature to observation *from within*," and few will deny the validity of his inference from this fact : " If the structure of the eye implies light, if the structure of the ear implies sound, then the structure of our conscience as certainly implies a spiritual presence and judgment, the access of some Being to our inward thoughts and motives."[2]

[1] " An *imperative* commands *hypothetically* or *categorically*. The former expresses that an action is necessary as a mean towards something further ; but the latter is such an *imperative* as represents an action to be in itself necessary and without regard had to anything out of and beyond it." —*Metaphysic of Ethics*, ch. ii.

[2] *Aspects of Religious and Scientific Thought*, p. 133.

Some theologians, who undervalue the moral argument for the existence of God, recognise the significance for the religious life of *the reproaches of conscience*. Ritschl does not hesitate to say that conscience may be described as the voice of God, and that " no man can be kept back from so interpreting reproaches of conscience "; but, as Professor Orr has pointed out, Ritschl has such a " dread of anything that bears the semblance of natural theology that he refuses to see in conscience an immediate witness for God." This is admitted by Mr. Garvie, who is, however, careful to show that Ritschl in his psychological analysis had no " intention to depreciate the value or authority of conscience."[1] It is true that men may not immediately recognise the voice that speaks within as " God's most intimate presence in the soul," but the problem is, Can the unique authority of conscience be retained when its origin is regarded as an open question ? Ritschl is right in maintaining that the revelation of God in conscience cannot be placed on an equality with the revelation of God in Christ; but this is frankly acknowledged by those who contend most earnestly that the " Power not ourselves that makes for righteousness," of whose reproaches man is conscious, is no abstraction but a personality. The final explanation of the accusations of conscience must surely be that God does not forsake those who put Him far from all their thoughts.

Ritschl's denial of the immediate divine origin of conscience appears to rest upon the assumption of *a false antithesis*. " The divine authority of the reproach of conscience cannot be understood as an immediate one, so long as an attempt to explain the matter from the spiritual essence or the moral

[1] *The Ritschlian Theology*, p. 87 f.

disposition of man has not been made, accordingly has not yet failed." But ethical philosophers who have most successfully attempted to explain the matter by a deeper analysis of man's moral nature cannot rest in the conclusion that Self is ultimate for thought; in the workings of conscience they trace the influences of the divine Spirit, and leave man in the depths of his moral being face to face with God. "What the critical intelligence labours to express takes shape for the ordinary intelligence in such phrases as 'the law of God written in men's hearts,' and 'the voice of God speaking through the human conscience.' Such phrases, however symbolical they may be, give utterance to the very deepest truth of moral obligation. They refer the idea of duty to its origin in man's own nature, and again trace that nature with all that is essential to it, to its origin in God."[1]

Man's sense of personal obligation remains as a "residual phenomenon" in spite of all attempts to explain it away; in the reproaches of conscience he hears not the voice of self-condemnation, but the voice of God; in the approval or disapproval of conscience he also becomes aware that "each shall bear his own burden" (Gal. vi. 5). "I have a centre of my own—a will of my own—which no one shares with me, nor can share,—a centre which I maintain even in my dealings with God Himself. . . . 'Our wills are ours to make them Thine,' but this is a *self*-surrender, a surrender which only self, only will can make."[2]

Herrmann's dislike of mysticism would be well founded

---

[1] D'Arcy, *Short Study of Ethics*, p. 142.
[2] Professor A. Seth, *Hegelianism and Personality*.

if its only idea of piety were " to forget self in gazing upon
the Eternal." But there are mystics *and* mystics ; if some
have taught that the end of religion is to lose one's self in
God, the ruling idea of others has been " I make the most
of myself for the sake of God." Communion with God is
no dreamy reverie in which the soul swoons away into
the unseen ; it is an act of the whole man, which always
demands his soul's collected powers, and which sometimes
calls for the exertion of all the strength of a strong will
in order that the wavering mind may be so fixed on things
divine as to intensify its desire : " Let all my powers
Thine entrance *feel*."

> How shall we have strength to glorify Him ?
> For He is Himself the great one above all His works.
> When ye glorify the Lord, exalt Him as much as ye can ;
> For even yet will He exceed :
> And when ye exalt Him, put forth your full strength.
> —ECCLUS. xliii. 28, 30.

In such communion devout souls gain deep insight into
the things of God ; their experience may be called mystical,
for they cannot fully explain to others all that with eyes
of faith they have clearly seen, but such mysticism is
essential to spiritual religion.

In communion between man and man there is *a mystical
element* ; as friend holds fellowship with friend, each gains
some real though not complete knowledge of the other.
Therefore, just as the analysis of man's spiritual nature
unfolds the meaning of " personality " and imparts knowledge of God, which is truth, though not the whole truth,
so by analogy we may learn from our methods of communion with each other, how God may impart and man

may receive knowledge of the divine mind and will, which though partial is trustworthy.

> Not e'en the tenderest heart, and next our own,
> Knows half the reasons why we smile and sigh !
> Each in his hidden sphere of joy or woe,
> Our hermit spirits dwell.[1]

Nevertheless, we know something of our friends; in communion with men of like nature with ourselves we acquire a more extended and more accurate knowledge both of our own personality and of theirs ; *if, then, we know ourselves and others, why may we not know God ?* If, as Dean Mansel taught, we are precluded from attaining to any real knowledge of God by the necessary laws of thought, we are incapable of knowing either our fellow-men or ourselves; but, on the other hand, if our knowledge of the mystery of " Self," though incomplete, is real, then our knowledge of God, who is high above our thought, may be real also. Dr. John Caird thus exposes the fallacy which underlies this familiar agnostic argument: " It does not follow that because we cannot know all, our partial knowledge is not therefore to be trusted ; that because human intelligence cannot comprehend God, it can have no real knowledge of Him. . . . Hopeless and universal indeed would be our ignorance, if that can never claim to be knowledge which is not perfect knowledge. . . . If, then, we feel that we *do* know something of our fellow-men, though we cannot know all, we conclude that our knowledge of God may be real though it cannot be exhaustive." [2]

How does man commune with man ? To ask the

[1] Keble.　　　[2] *The Fundamental Ideas of Christianity*, lvii.

question is to remind ourselves that our communion with our friends is spiritual, and that the real question is, *How does mind commune with mind?* A work of art is an expression of the artist's mind; the man appears in his *work,* so that the material form acquires a spiritual significance. To the students of the Royal Academy, Sir Frederick Leighton could say, " Whatever noble fire is in our hearts will burn also in our work ; whatever purity is ours will chasten and exalt it ; for as we are, so our work is."

But *words* are the most frequent media of communication between mind and mind; " a word fitly spoken," well chosen and in due season, is sufficient to convey true knowledge to the wise. Sir Fitzjames Stephen expresses the exact truth in a fine simile : " Words on the highest subjects must be used as signals made by spirits in prison to each other, with a world of things to think and to say which our signals cannot describe at all." It is suggestive that this recognition of the mystical element in human speech should come from a distinguished lawyer accustomed to the sifting of evidence and to careful discrimination of the exact meaning of words. Words may indeed " half conceal " as well as " half reveal " the thoughts of the heart, and in the most confidential intercourse there are moments when words altogether fail—moments which are nevertheless moments of revealing as in silence the heart listens. " *Silence unto God,*" as the Hebrew psalmists had learnt, is one way of waiting upon God. But this silence is not the silence of aloofness and inaction, like one of those awkward pauses in friendly intercourse which are the result of scanty knowledge of topics of mutual interest ; it is a silence in which only those find blessing who have been wont in unreserved confidences " to pour out their hearts " (Ps. lxii. 8) ; nor is the silence an end in itself, as though the more unconscious the soul became, the more complete were its felicity ; it is rather the silence that waits for further revealing of the Beloved's thoughts in reposeful trust which no questioning of His constancy can disturb ; this *silence involves effort*, the hushing of the clamour of discordant desires, the bringing into captivity of unruly thoughts, and the resolute reconciling of every conflicting interest in calm submission to His will.

> Rapt into still communion which transcends
> The imperfect offices of prayers and praise,
> *The mind is a thanksgiving* to the Power
> Which made it. It is blessedness and love.[1]

The psalmist, whose soul is already " silence unto God " (Ps. lxii. 1, R.V. margin), is compelled to exhort his soul to maintain this spiritual calm, " unto God be thou silent " (ver. 5) ; and his reward is to hear the silence broken not once only, but twice :

> God hath spoken once,
> Twice have I heard this ;
> That power belongeth unto God :
> Also unto Thee, O Lord, belongeth mercy.
> —Ps. lxii. 11, 12.

Apart, however, from the fact that words of truth do not always express all the truth, words may be used with intent to deceive ; even then " the hidden man of the heart " is revealed by some glance of the eye or some slight gesture, so that whenever the life contradicts the lips we do well to say " *actions* speak louder than words." Hence if a

[1] Wordsworth, *The Excursion*.

5

man's work, his words, and above all his life, reveal the thoughts and imaginations of his heart, we may expect to find *the mind of God revealed in His works and in His deeds*, i.e. in Nature and in History; but we shall not be surprised at the discovery that " these are but the outskirts of His ways." " How small a whisper do we hear of Him " (Job xxvi. 14, R.V.) until we listen to His beloved Son, whose words " are spirit and are life " (John vi. 63), because He is Himself the Word of God incarnate, and the Life and Light of men.

Inasmuch, then, as communion is reciprocal and spirit must respond to spirit, our own experience should teach us that just as true love gives deeper insight into character than a keen intellect, so *our knowledge of God is conditioned by our spiritual attainments* rather than by our mental gifts.

> Learn that to love is the one way to know
> Or God or man.[1]

A moment's reflection will convince us that there are very few persons whom we really know. How often our own narrow souls have led us to form misconceptions and perhaps to express false judgments of some noble character. Mr. Illingworth, in his most instructive chapter on " Moral Affinity needful for Knowledge of a Person," analyses with great skill the process of acquiring such knowledge : " We may easily idolise or underestimate a man, but to know him as he is—his true motives, the secret springs of his conduct—this is often a work of years, and one in which our own character and conduct play quite as important

[1] Jean Ingelow.

a part as our understanding : for not only must the necessary insight be the result of our own acquired capacities, but there must further exist the kind and degree of affinity between us which can alone make self-revelation on his part possible. . . . A man cannot understand a character with which his own has no accord. And affinity with a Holy Being implies a progressive and lifelong effort of the will."[1]   To abbreviate this carefully reasoned argument from analogy is to do it injustice ; but the few sentences quoted here, before we consider how God has made Himself known to men, should lead us to reflect that it may be the veil upon our own hearts which is preventing us from beholding the brightness of His glory.   Before we cry for more light, let us be sure that in this sense Tennyson's words are not true of us :

Dark is the world to thee? Thyself art the reason why.[2]

---

[1] *Personality*, pp. 117, 121.   [2] *Higher Pantheism.*

Chapter the Fifth

THE REVELATION OF GOD IN NATURE

For the invisible things of Him since the creation of the world are clearly seen, being perceived through the things that are made, even His everlasting power and divinity.—Rom. i. 20 (R.V.).

> His most holy name is Love,
> Truth of subliming import! with the which
> Who feeds and saturates his constant soul,
> He from his small particular orbit flies
> With blest outstarting! From himself he flies,
> Stands in the sun, and with no partial gaze
> Views all creation: and he loves it all
> And blesses it, and calls it very good.

PERSONALITY, as we know it in ourselves and others, includes *the power of self-revelation.* "Even a child"—whose character is not fully formed, but who has not learnt to dissemble,—"even a child maketh himself known by his doings" (Prov. xx. 11, R.V.). Hence the belief that God, as a personal Spirit, reveals in the visible creation His invisible attributes, commends itself to the reason of men who know that through imperfect media true knowledge of their inmost thoughts may be conveyed to other minds.

The analogy between the revelation of human personality in words or in deeds and the revelation of God in Nature will prepare us to find that in Nature God may be unable to reveal all the knowledge of Himself that He desires to impart. Theology and Psychology must both confess that

> Words—like Nature—half reveal
> And half conceal the soul within.

Yet, " assuming good faith, we never regard a man's acts and utterances as masking, but rather as manifesting the man. If they mask when it is his intention to deceive, surely they cannot also mask when his intentions are the precise opposite. These acts and utterances may be beyond the comprehension of men on a lower intellectual level, and with narrower horizons, but they are not the less real or true on that account. And why should we argue differently when reflection leads us to see in a universe declared to be 'everywhere alive' the manifestations of a supreme Mind."[1]

> The things of earth
> Are copies of the things in heaven, more close,
> More clear, more near, more intricately linked,
> More subtle than men guess. Mysterious—
> Finger on lip—whispering to wistful ears,
> Nature doth shadow spirit.[2]

In modern thought the tendency has been to rush from one extreme to another—from the extreme of regarding Nature's teachings as alone sufficient for man's moral guidance, to the extreme of neglecting altogether Nature's ministry to man's spiritual life. The old Deistic teaching has been revived by popular novelists, who have not only declared that " Nature is the true revelation of the Deity to man," but have also bidden us *go to Nature to learn our morals*, as though the Cynics and their successors in all

---

[1] Ward, *Naturalism and Agnosticism*, vol. ii. p. 276.
[2] Sir E. Arnold, *The Light of the World*, p. 171.

ages had not made it perfectly plain that under this cloak all forms of foul shamelessness may hide. The opposite extreme of thought is represented by the Ritschlian school, which unduly depreciates Nature's teachings and refers us to the inner life of Jesus as the sole revelation of God. As making against both these tendencies there may be noted a greater readiness to discern spiritual law in the natural world, to cease from magnifying the differences between natural and revealed religion, and to go back to the position of Clement of Alexandria : " I know of no distinction between what man discovers and what God reveals." Of His own *words* Jesus said, " The Father abiding in Me doeth His *works* " (John xiv. 10, R.V.); but He also declared that in the universe His Father had been at work from the Creation " until now " (John v. 17, R.V.). There cannot be any ultimate contradiction between the work of the Father as revealed in Nature and as revealed in Christ, "through whom He made the worlds " (Heb. i. 2, R.V.). Our wisdom, as Bishop Lightfoot reminds us, is to " connect Christ with the marvels of Creation, with the laws of Nature, with the progress and development of History. Would not the average Christian be startled," he asks, " if he were told that the laws of gravitation, of chemical affinity, of magnetism were expressions of the mind of Christ? But the Father manifests Himself through the Eternal Word not in revelation only but in nature, not in redemption only but in history . . . all the threads of scientific laws are gathered up in the hands of Him who is the centre of our faith and the foundation of our hope."

There are two views of natural religion which fail to

account for the facts of the Christian consciousness and which are subversive of spiritual religion. *Nature is sometimes personified and made a synonym for God :* instead of a personal Deity to whom prayer and praise can be offered, we have a vague abstraction with which communion is inconceivable. Scientists know that when the word " Nature " is so used, no definite statement can be made about it ; but owing to this haziness of thought it is possible, according to the fancy of the writer, to represent Nature as *cruel* in order that the divine justice may be impugned, or as *kindly* in order that society's adverse verdicts may be evaded, on the ground that sins which are severely judged by men are not condemned by Nature. Some modern writers say " Nature " when our fathers would have said " God," but Nature thus becomes the negation and not a synonym of God. Dr. Martineau forcefully protests against a similar abuse of the time-honoured expression, *Natural Religion* : to-day as of old natural religion ought to mean " the teachings of nature about God," not " the substitution of nature for God . . . in other words, Nature-worship in place of divine worship." [1]

Another view of natural religion which is destructive alike of spiritual religion and of morals *exaggerates the value of Nature's teachings* in order that a supernatural revelation may appear superfluous. Bishop Butler's reply to those who in his day maintained that Christianity added nothing to natural religion is by no means antiquated: the difficulties that beset " natural " religion are as formidable and as numerous as the difficulties that beset " revealed " religion. How invulnerable this argument still is, the frank avowal of a modern writer sufficiently proves : " The

[1] *A Study of Religion,* vol. i. p. 6 f.

root of the moral difficulty is that the natural world is
non-moral, and the natural world is all we have to appeal
to when the various forms of the supernatural have all
equally been rejected." [1]　The Naturalism which sends us
to " the nearest green field " to read from its " inspired
page " all that we need to know of God, stifles prayer and
undermines the foundations of morals. " Nature cares
nothing for the ideas of the New Testament as to the family,"
says Renan ; but Mr. Matthew Arnold has exposed the
fallacy of this and every like statement : " Instead of saying
that Nature cares nothing about chastity, let us say that
human nature, *our* nature, cares about it a great deal." [2]
It is wise to remember that natural laws apply to man
because he is part of Nature ; it is foolish to forget that he
is subject also to spiritual laws which do not apply to plants
and animals whose nature he transcends.

> Know, man hath all which Nature hath, but more,
> And in that *more* lie all his hopes of good.
> Man must begin, know this, where Nature ends ;
> Nature and man can never be fast friends. [3]

The *reductio ad absurdum* of Naturalism is seen in the
unblushing Egoism and Materialism of Nietzsche, whose
writings are not without influence in our own country.
It has long been recognised that man is a " bundle of contradictions " ; it would be necessary also to recognise that
" the frenzy of centuries breaks out in him," if it were a fact
that the " only fairly successful man " is the " primitive
blond beast, the beast of prey, without a conscience and
a faith, save the unhesitating faith in his instincts." It is

---

[1] P. G. Hamerton.　　　　　[2] *Discourses in America : Numbers.*
[3] Matthew Arnold, *In Harmony with Nature.*

well to see clearly whither such teaching leads. *If "everything good is instinct,"* and *if* the "so-called motive" is
"only a surface-phenomenon of consciousness," then, but
not till then, will men believe that "the home of our true
being and of our best wisdom is our body," that "our mind
is but an interloper," and that "we take a nervous or
stomachic uneasiness and describe it in terms of morals
and religion, as, *e.g.*, guilt or sin." Neither the word
"natural" nor the word "religion" can legitimately be applied
to any theory which contains such a "draught of human
nature" as this. All history confirms St. Paul's judgment that instincts and passions unbridled by conscience
lead to crimes which are "against nature"; and to speak
either of nature or of matter as being of necessity antago-
nistic to spirit is to degrade language.

Spiritual natures hold *communion with each other by
means of matter and its modifications,* and this is the highest
use to which spirit can put material which it alone can
make expressive of thought. Hence, if by nature is meant
the material universe, the relation of nature to spirit—
human and divine—can scarcely be more accurately defined
than in Professor Iverach's words: "Nature is the middle
term between God and man, an instrument in the hand
of both for communion and knowledge." [1]

> This is the glory,—that in all conceived,
> Or felt, or known, I recognise a mind,
> Not mine but like mine,—for the double joy,—
> Making all things for me and me for Him. [2]

Wordsworth has given classic expression to the influence

[1] *Theism in the Light of Present Science and Philosophy*, p. 315.
[2] Robert Browning, *Prince Hohenstiel Schwangan.*

which material nature exerts on the human spirit ; and Mr. Illingworth, by a series of typical illustrations selected from ancient and modern literature, proves that this influence has been " in all ages of the world, and under every variety of culture and creed . . . a main influence making for religion. . . . Thus matter has, as a fact, from the very dawn of human history, ministered to the religious development of spirit." [1] Spiritual religion has never been promoted by the undervaluing of this ministry. History should teach us that whenever the study of Nature has been condemned as harmful to the spiritual well-being of man, a reaction has been provoked ; as in the eighteenth century when the religion of Nature was exalted to a preeminence which ultimately proved prejudicial to the interests of all religion, whether natural or revealed.

It startles us to read that St. Bernard rode a whole day along the shores of Lake Leman with downcast eyes, " lest the created beauty of the scene should tempt his soul from interior contemplation," or that St. Augustine " cursed the light, that queen of colours, for distracting him from prayer." [2] Such examples, however, prove that in spite of a false theory Nature appealed to those spiritually-minded men. The mental attitude in which devout men contemplate Nature in modern times is better represented by Jacobi's words to his friend Wizenmann, as they were sitting in the garden : " I often sit here watching the setting sun, and think with what rapture I should be filled if a miracle of grace were to assure me of his existence. Then I stand up on fire with the thought—God ! and feel as if I should

---

[1] *Divine Immanence*, ch. ii.
[2] Algar Thorold, *Catholic Mysticism*, p. 81.

like to call together the whole world to preach God to it. *No chaos could possess the power to move me thus.*" [1]

In the temple of Nature where " everything saith Glory," the spirit of man listens to " the voice of the Lord "; and because that voice is " full of majesty " man gives unto the Lord " the glory due unto His name," and worships the Lord " in the beauty of holiness " (Ps. xxix. 2, 9). No philosophy of religion can claim to offer an explanation of the facts of the spiritual consciousness if such testimonies are ignored ; the experience therein described is neither rare nor isolated, and it is an experience which others may verify. The witness of the starry heavens to the glory of God is a universal proclamation, like the glad tidings of salvation ; " unto the end of the world " both messages go forth ; and the fact that all do not hearken casts doubt neither on the reality of Nature's revelation of God's glory, nor on the credibility of the Gospel revelation of His grace (Ps. xix. 5 ; cf. Rom. x. 18).   Such an experience as Coleridge relates has often been repeated as men have lifted up their eyes unto the mountains :

> O dread and silent mount ! I gazed upon thee
> Till thou, still present to the bodily sense,
> Didst vanish from my thought ; entranced in prayer
> I worshipped the Invisible alone.[2]

Ruskin's beautiful description of the formation of the Matter-horn cliffs by " the axe of God " out of " the little flakes of mica sand . . . kneaded into a strength as of imperishable iron, rustless by the air, infusible by the flame," may serve to show that the scientific study of Nature, so far

---

[1] Höffding, *History of Modern Philosophy*, vol. ii. p. 575.
[2] *Hymn before Sunrise in the Vale of Chamouni.*

from being incompatible with religious. contemplation, may promote it. " We shall find that the love of Nature, wherever it has existed, has been a faithful and sacred element of feeling ; that is to say, supposing all the circumstances otherwise the same with respect to two individuals, the one who loves Nature most will be always found to have more capacity for faith in God than the other. Natureworship [1] will be found to bring with it such a sense of the presence and power of a Great Spirit as no mere reasoning can either induce or controvert." [2]

Opinions may differ as to whether with increased facilities for exploring the beauties of Nature the majority of men are becoming more responsive to her highest teachings, but none can doubt that the outlook for spiritual religion in the twentieth century is far more hopeful because Wordsworth taught so many of the most influential thinkers of the nineteenth century to

> live
> By sensible impressions not enthralled,
> But by their quickening impulse made more prompt
> To hold fit converse with the spiritual world.[3]

It is true that " converse with the spiritual world is not necessarily communion with God as a personal Spirit, but when to " the ear of faith " the Universe has whispered " authentic tidings of invisible things," the soul will become more quick to hear, in " the still sad music of humanity," the voice of the divine Spirit, " whose dwelling is the light of setting suns . . . *and in the mind of man.*" Such

[1] Cp. Dr. Martineau's protest (p. 71) against the degradation of this expression.

[2] *Modern Painters.* See *Frondes Agrestes*, §§ 8, 62.

[3] *The Ascent of Snowdon.*

recognition of " the Power that made him," though it falls far short of the all-sufficing knowledge of the Father, may prepare a devout spirit to learn that the crowning manifestation of God is neither in Nature nor in Man, but in the " Son of His love," in whom " it was the good pleasure of the Father that all the fulness should dwell " (Col. i. 19, R.V.).

In the study of Nature, Science and Art may be handmaids of spiritual religion. Scientific interest in natural phenomena is not lessened by a desire to gain insight into the truth of God ; nor is æsthetic enjoyment of the sublime scenes which Nature spreads before the eye of the artist less thrilling because he has learnt to contemplate the light as " the garment of God " and the clouds as His " chariots " (Ps. civ. 2 f.). The *Nature Psalms* are the expression not of scientific but of religious truth ; they were written by men whose spiritual emotions were profoundly stirred, hence they are sung to-day by reverent scientists who have a more accurate knowledge of Nature's processes, and by devout artists who have truer perceptions of Nature's beauties than these saints of old ; the time will never come when these inspired words will cease to be a fitting expression for those sacred experiences in which the soul communes with God whilst musing on the work of His hands. Dean Church has compared the Hebrew Psalms with the sacred poetry of the heathen religions, and in so doing has cast light upon the nature of the psalmists' inspiration. In their " lightning-like glimpses of spiritual truth " there is " something more than the mere working of the mind of man . . . they repeat the whispers of the Spirit of God and reflect the very light of the Eternal Wisdom." Hence whilst the Vedic hymns are dead, " the Psalms are as living as when they were written . . . they were composed in an age at least as immature as that of the singers of the Veda, but they are now what they have been for thirty centuries, the very life of spiritual religion." [1]

It is, however, *in the words of his Lord and Master* that the Christian student of Nature will look for the clearest light on the connexion between the natural and the spiritual world; nor will he look in vain. Before Jesus "opened the book" in the synagogue at Nazareth and announced that in Him the ancient Scriptures were fulfilled, He had in His conversation with Nicodemus compared the influences of the Spirit to the action of the wind, and He had spoken to the woman of Samaria of "the living water" and of the spiritual "harvest" of which her faith was the first-fruits (John iii. 8, iv. 35). Thus the earliest recorded sayings of Christ reveal a mind accustomed to read the open book of Nature, and to trace in its familiar processes analogies to spiritual truth. If, as is probable, His brethren James and Jude are the authors of the epistles which bear their respective names, we may reverently think of the children in the home at Nazareth as learning to love Nature and to observe her ways. The similes of James are frequently derived from rural life: the flower withering away under the burning sun suggested to him thoughts of the transitory nature of earthly prosperity, and the disappearing mist became an emblem of human life (Jas. i. 11, iv. 14). Jude too had watched the clouds drift past without watering the earth, and had marked the tree which in the autumn

[1] *The Sacred Poetry of Early Religions*, p. 38.

bore no fruit; these and other graphic metaphors impart force and beauty to his description of the character of hypocrites who had crept into the Church (Jude 12, R.V.).

But whatever be the truth in regard to "the brethren of the Lord," there can be no doubt that in those years when Jesus was advancing in wisdom, Nature was to His "pure eyes" imparting heavenly truth. When our Lord formally began His ministry and in the *Sermon on the Mount* taught His disciples "how to pray," He also gave them commandment to "behold the birds" and to "consider the lilies of the field" (Matt. vi. 9, 26 f.). To pray aright it cannot therefore be needful to shut the eyes to the beauties of Nature; on the contrary, Jesus would have us learn from "the grass of the field" to cast aside the anxious care which is inconsistent with the true spirit of prayer (Matt. vi. 31; cp. Phil. iv. 6). Nevertheless, whilst bidding His disciples learn such lessons from Nature, Jesus was careful to direct their attention to the *difference* between "the birds of the heaven" or "the lilies of the field" and the children of the heavenly Father who, in the hour of need, can ask Him for "good things" and for the Holy Spirit, who in the inward life is the all-comprising good (Matt. vii. 11; cp. Luke xi. 13). "Of how much more value" than the birds and the lilies are spiritual beings who in childlike trust and humble gratitude can cast all their care on God? He feeds the birds and clothes the lilies, and will therefore be *much more* willing to supply His children's needs.

Our Lord's use of natural metaphors is proof not only of His delight in Nature, but also of His consciousness of *the limitations of Nature's teachings*. He saw the "invisible things" of God—His power and wisdom and goodness—

revealed in the sunshine and the shower, in the cornfield, the vineyard, and the orchard ; His parables drawn from the material world set forth the principles which determine the spread of His kingdom amongst men, but the straining of language in His own expositions (cp. the recurring phrase " *he* that was sown," Matt. xiii. 19, etc.) of their meaning shows that Nature is not a perfect image of grace. For example, the mutual influences upon each other of the seed and the soil cannot adequately represent the effect of the divine word upon human hearts ; in the kingdom of nature the soil cannot rid itself of thorns and stones, whereas in the kingdom of grace the purifying of the soul is conditional on willing obedience to the truth (1 Pet. i. 22) ; in the kingdom of nature the seed has no power to change the soil, whereas in the kingdom of grace the word of truth renews the nature, and when rooted deep within and "mixed with faith " saves the soul (Jas. i. 18 f.; cp. Heb. iv. 2). It was not to Nature that Jesus sent His disciples to learn their duty and their responsibility as moral and spiritual beings, hence the majority of His parables are drawn from the relations of man to his fellow-men. How contrary to His teachings are all the various forms of Naturalism ! Between Him and ourselves there was, moreover, this great difference : He had no consciousness of sin, therefore to Him the thought of God was always welcome. The Sinless One had no desire to hide from God's face among the trees of the garden; it was never any effort for Him to "rise from Nature up to Nature's God." Christ's communion with His Father was unaffected by the fact that Nature cannot assure the sinner that the thoughts of God are thoughts of peace. The condition upon which we may share the experience of Him who never tried to put God far from all His thoughts is laid down in His own words, " No one cometh unto the Father, but by Me" (John xiv. 6, R.V.).

The seeker after God, who is bewildered by the study of the arguments for the divine existence, does wisely in following the counsel of those who bid him " return to Christ" in order that at His feet those lessons of spiritual wisdom and grace may be learnt which cannot be acquired by the most diligent study in the school of Nature ; but from the presence of Christ His disciple may " return to Nature" to be instructed in her mystic lore, willing to learn from the wild flowers and the worthless sparrow in the lowly spirit of a child, who now

> Can lift to heaven an unpresumptuous eye,
> And smiling say, "My Father made them all."[1]

In the visible creation men have discovered revelations of a supreme Mind and Will, in spiritual experience Christians have also learnt that the revelation of God in His Son is the climax, but not the contradiction, of His revelation in Nature. Such facts are faith's sufficient warrant for asserting that Nature ministers to the spiritual life of men. But some never pass from the light of Nature into the presence of the Light of life ; hence although their understandings are illuminated they are tormented by the soul's " hunger for more light," and in gloomy hours when the conscience craves peace and the troubled heart sighs for rest, they complain that from the face of Nature all the smiles have vanished. To the questions which rise from the depths

[1] Cowper, *The Task*, Book v.

of man's spiritual being, *Nature can give no clear and un-ambiguous answer* ; " now it reveals to you, in the mechanics and physics of the stars, or in the processes of living beings, vast realms of marvellous reasonableness ; now it bewilders you in the endless diversity of natural facts, by a chaos of unintelligible fragments and of scattered events; now it lifts up your heart with wondrous glimpses of ineffable goodness ; and now it arouses your wrath by frightful signs of cruelty and baseness." [1]

Very pathetic are some of the confessions of one who was gifted with rare insight into Nature's beauty and who, by travel and study, had highly developed his artistic gifts. Mr. J. A. Symonds speaks of moments when life appeared to be " a mountain-chasm filled with tumbling mists, and whether there be Alps and flowers and streams below and snows above, with stars or sunlight in the sky, I do not see. I want faith ; I have no faith, not even in myself." Once he despairingly cries, " I have found Hell in this terrestrial Paradise ; I have ceased to believe in Paradise "; but, as a rule, he blames himself; and not Nature: "Some clear faith in things that are good and true and pure and eternal would make all the difference." And to this heroic soul who refused to " dull the pangs of the present " by using Hasheesh, some clear faith was given, for he writes : " Hasheesh is good for a season, but this is no solution of the problem. Therefore to whom turn I but to Thee, the ineffable Name ? Ever onwards towards Infinity I voyage, demanding only what is permanent, imperishable, in the world of reality "; and on the last New Year's Eve

---

[1] Royce, *The World and the Individual* (Gifford Lectures, 1899), p. 17.

of his life: "God is over all. That is what the tolling bells are saying to me this night. God is over all."[1]

The ministry of Nature to the spiritual life of man is not a delusion because of the disappointment of those who have sought in converse with Nature what can only be found in communion with God through Christ. Man must be at peace with the God of Nature, or its higher harmonies will be unheard; to see God he must be pure in heart; to learn wisdom from the powers of Nature that fulfil His word, "their glorious tasks in silence perfecting," he must have a will to do God's will.

> O God! I
> Can see no beauty on this beauteous earth,
> No life, no light, no hopefulness, no mirth,
>   Pleasure nor purpose, where Thou art not nigh.
> But when Thy feet flutter the dark, and Thou
>   With orient eyes dawnest on my distress,
> Suddenly sings a bird on every bough,
>   The heavens expand, the earth grows less and less,
> The ground is buoyant as the ether now,
>   And all looks lovely in Thy loveliness.[2]

---

[1] John Addington Symonds, *A Biography*, vol. i. p. 416 f.; vol. ii. p. 226 f.

[2] Alfred Austin.

Chapter the Sixth

THE REVELATION OF GOD IN HISTORY

Yet God is my King of old,
Working salvation in the midst of the earth.
—Ps. lxxiv. 12 (R.V.).

When I look over my entire life and contemplate history in all its branches, then I am a believer in God with all my heart; any other theory of the world is to me unintelligible.—LEOPOLD VON RANKE.

DIFFICULT as it is to characterise the intellectual life of a century, there is little risk of hasty generalisation in saying that the greatest advances in knowledge during the nineteenth century were the result of the application of *the historic method* to all branches of scientific and philosophical study. The expression "philosophy of history," which Hegel's great work has made familiar, implies that rational principle and not caprice guides the development of tendencies and the progress of events. Such a conception of history accords well with the religious view of the world; for if Nature be the expression of the supreme Mind and Will, there is at least a strong presumption that in the course of human affairs the divine purpose will be gradually unfolded, and the same facts which are regarded by the scientific historian as evidences of the moral advancement of the race may be conversely viewed by the theistic philosopher as a revelation of the character of God.

The Science of History, so long as it keeps within its proper sphere, offers neither a naturalistic nor a theistic solution of the world-problems which its researches bring to light. Much confusion of thought would be prevented and much prejudice would be removed, if it were generally recognised that to the *Science* of History belong the observation, the classification, and the recording of facts, whilst to the *Philosophy* of History is committed the higher and more arduous task of explaining them by interpreting the tendencies of which they were the outcome. It is the naturalistic hypotheses of historical criticism and not the attested results of historical investigation which are destructive of the foundations of spiritual religion. Both the *philosophy of history* and the *philosophy of religion* must take account of the facts brought to light by the scientific Evolutionist, as he traces complex existences back to their simpler forms. But no scientific induction from facts warrants the assertion that the highest types of religion are derived from crude superstitions ; indeed, the inclusion of Christianity within the domain of natural history involves an assumption in direct violation of the great principle which, as Hegel taught, makes history intelligible : that it is the fully developed form which reveals the latent potentialities of the germ.[1] " You may create a so-called science of history by forcing spiritual realities through the sieve of natural law ; but in so doing you have left out the very elements which differentiated man from nature. . . . It is because man is a spirit and not

[1] Cp. Aristotle's definition of the *nature* of a thing as its condition when the process of production is complete. ἡ φύσις τέλος ἐστίν· οἷον γὰρ ἕκαστόν ἐστι τῆς γενέσεως τελεσθείσης, ταύτην φαμὲν τὴν φύσιν εἶναι ἑκάστου, ὥσπερ ἀνθρώπου, ἵππου, οἰκίας.—*Politics*, I. ii. 1252.

an animal that history is the record of a progress to which the biological expert has no key." [1]

Between writers who recognise the hand of God in human history there may be great differences of opinion in regard to the genuineness of ancient documents or the trustworthiness of some of the biblical narratives; still greater differences may emerge when a distinction is drawn between eternal truth and the contemporary garb (*Zeitgewand*) in which God has revealed it to us; but the principal line of cleavage is between those who accept *a naturalistic view of the world* and those who find it impossible to believe that the life of humanity is but

> the fretful foam
> Of vehement action without scope or term
> Called History. [2]

The main issue is well stated by Dr. Harnack; in a review of a "Natural History of the Christian Doctrine" he says, "I am unable to accept as sufficient in the history of religion the common religious instinct working under the influence of natural forces and amid historical conditions." New light upon historical conditions, it may confidently be said, is making it increasingly difficult to believe that common instincts are the source of spiritual religion, unless common instinct be a name for the human response to the divine Spirit.

In recent years the interests of spiritual religion have

---

[1] Dr. John Caird, *University Addresses*, p. 257 f.

[2] Shelley describes history as a "record of crimes and miseries, . . . a study that is hateful and disgusting to my very soul." But his avowal should be noted : "Facts are not what we want to know in poetry, in history." See Dowden, *Studies in Literature*, ch. iii.

been promoted by the historic study of human nature as well as by the scientific study of human history in general. The history of religious beliefs is part of the history of the race, and very significant is the fact, which few anthropologists would now deny, that *the religious instinct is a universal attribute of man*. " Little by little," says De Quatrefages, " the light has appeared, and the result has been that Australians, Melanesians, Bosjesmans, Hottentots, Kaffirs, and Bechuanas have in their turn been withdrawn from the list of atheist nations and recognised as religious." Even Professor Tylor, who thinks that " nothing in the nature of things seems to forbid the possibility of the existence of non-religious tribes as of tribes without language," frankly owns " that as a matter of fact the tribes are not found." Herein it is permissible to find strong confirmation of the belief

> that in all ages
> Every human heart is human,
> That in even savage bosoms
> There are longings, yearnings, strivings
> For the good they comprehend not,
> That the feeble hands and helpless,
> Groping blindly in the darkness,
> Touch God's right hand in that darkness
> And are lifted up and strengthened.[1]

That the poet has seen into the heart of things let the Evolutionist bear witness. Dr. Fiske hesitates to attribute personality to the Deity, but his words are in harmony with the fuller statement of the divine purpose, as revealed in Scripture and as confirmed in every soul that knows the joys of spiritual religion and finds therein his being's end and aim : " As a general thing in the whole history

[1] Longfellow, *Song of Hiawatha.*

of Evolution, when you see any internal adjustment reaching out toward something, it is in order to adapt itself to something that really exists ; and if the religious cravings of man constitute an exception they are the one thing in the whole process of Evolution that is exceptional and different from all the rest. And this is surely an argument of stupendous and resistless weight." [1]

The Science of Religion, which was a product of the nineteenth century, has in the course of its researches made us acquainted with many curious rites in which the religious instinct of man has found expression, but " man's sense of the divine always carried the thought of moving the God in some way, of communicating with Him, and in return receiving signs or revealings of His will. . . . Assurance of *the reality of communion with the divine* underlies all the fantastic, unimaginable shapes in which mankind in different stages have sought to avail themselves of the guidance and succour of their Gods." [2] There is therefore no reason why, as historical knowledge increases, our faith should not be confirmed ; Christianity satisfies the test that the higher form of religion must explain the lower ; it has a response for all man's spiritual cravings ; and it realises all that was good in ancient ideals. The study of primitive creeds and of early forms of worship confirms the truth of the words of Jesus : If God, who " is spirit," is drawing men to worship Him in accordance with reality, the reachings out of man's spirit after God are fully accounted for ; they prove not merely that man has always been

---

[1] *A Century of Science*, p. 115.
[2] Taylor, *Ancient Ideals*, vol. ii. p. 400.

seeking God, but that the Father has always been seeking men (John iv. 23 f.).

Professor de la Saussaye, the accomplished author of a well known *Manual of the Science of Religion*, thus summarises the results of the studies of many years: "The pearls of religious poetry, the prayers to Varuna in the Rig-Veda, the Assyrian penitential Psalms, the choruses of the Greek tragic poets, the blossomings of Persian-Mohammedan Mysticism, and what more shall I mention?—here and there also among semi-barbarians and savages the utterances of a piety with which we can sympathise,—these all testify to the religious necessities of mankind. Men serve God even when they do not know Him,—the living God, who is not far from the nations, whom He regards as they walk in their own ways." [1]

The gradual evolution of *more spiritual conceptions of God* is a fact patent to all students of Comparative Religion, however they may differ in their inferences from it. So far, however, from proving that the idea of a Supreme Being is of human origin, this fact rather suggests that men have been divinely guided in a search which would otherwise have been a mere groping in the dark. Some elements of truth may be discerned in the most primitive conceptions of God, some germs of reverence in the rudest forms of worship. From lowly beginnings and in spite of surroundings which tended to debase and materialise his aspirations, man has advanced so far as to conceive of God as a personal spirit with whom he may hold communion: this fact is inexplicable on the assumption that in the evolution of

[1] *Die vergleichende Religionsforschung und der religiöse Glaube*, p. 26.

religion man was left to his own heart's imaginings. His progress in divine knowledge has sometimes been by painful steps and slow; the story is a record of advance, marred by frequent relapses. But the explanation of these facts is not far to seek, for it is on moral qualities and on spiritual insight that man's apprehension of the revelation of God is conditional.

One clear gain has resulted from historical inquiries into pre-Christian religions. *A preparation in history for Christ amongst Gentile nations* is acknowledged without any hesitation. Five centuries before Christ Confucius had formulated a golden rule: "What you do not wish done to yourself do not do to others." A century later Socrates was endeavouring to raise the tone of Athenian morals by his noble teaching that the chief good of life and its highest pleasures are attained by those who are conscious that their earnest endeavours after self-improvement have been successful.[1] It is as unjust to call the virtues upon which Socrates discoursed "splendid vices," as it is unwise to describe him in Shelley's phrase as "the. Jesus Christ of Greece." To ascribe due honour to such seekers after wisdom and preachers of righteousness is not to imperil but to render more secure the position of Christ on His historic throne. Tertullian said, "The Christian child has understanding of truths hidden from the philosophers"; his words are true because the least in the kingdom of God is greater than the greatest of those who could but say "the kingdom is at hand."

---

[1] Cp. Xenophon, *Memorabilia*, iv. 8. § 6. Ἄριστα ζῆν τοὺς ἄριστα ἐπιμελομένους τοῦ ὡς βελτίστους γίγνεσθαι, ἥδιστα δὲ τοὺς μάλιστα αἰσθανομένους ὅτι βελτίους γίγνονται.

The Christian child walks in the light that is broadening to noon, but these old-world sages were feeling after God in the dim twilight that precedes the dawn. Before the sun is visible above the horizon, the topmost peaks are illumined by his rays : the light that was in these ancient teachers was not all darkness, for in the ages before His Incarnation the Eternal Word was " the light that lighteth every man " (John i. 4). " The faith of non-Christians is not," says Dr. Hort, "in the strict sense, faith in Jesus Christ . . . but such faith, when ripened, grows into the faith of Jesus Christ. . . . All the good there is in the world is what one may call imperfect Christianity, not as something essentially different, requiring so to speak to be dealt with by God in a wholly different manner." [1]

But passing from the comparative study of religious phenomena we have still to consider the relation to faith of the facts which present themselves to the philosophic student of human history in general. In the literature of nations whose chronicles and whose poetry make no claim to be a divine revelation, such students discover evidences of the working of a Power that makes for righteousness, and some of them do not hesitate to say that they find *God in the history*, although it was not written from this point of view. As the long-hidden records of the rise and fall of empires leap to light, men behold written large upon them the everlasting law of right. The revelation of God in history is not dependent upon the inspiration of men to write the verbal narrative of the divine guidance of a nation's career. But the conscious and undisguised purpose of an

[1] *Life and Letters*, vol. ii. p. 337.

historian may be to show that a divine hand directed a nation's course and controlled its destiny; moreover, his narrative may convince its readers that he was inspired of God to write the record of His dealings with His people.

Such a record we have in *the Old Testament Scriptures*. The history of Israel is no mere chronicle of human folly and human wisdom, nor is it a narrative of a people's gradual but unaided development in morals and religion; it is the story of "the deeds of the Lord." If in what is called profane history a divine and unifying purpose may be discerned, we may expect to find in sacred history that the main object of the writer is to trace the manifestations of that purpose, nor should his plain avowal that his narrative is written from this point of view arouse any prejudice against the trustworthiness of his recital of the facts. The scientist, who records without interpreting the facts of history, is obliged to speak of an "aim" and of an "end" of the cosmic process, but a philosophy of history is necessary in order that his words may become intelligible; such a philosophy is found in the Bible. From Genesis to Revelation God rules the history, and this, as Dr. A. B. Davidson points out, is at once the explanation of the history and the reason for recording it: "It is of God, not of men, that the Bible speaks. . . . God has been in the history of mankind from the beginning. . . . The Old Testament was religious experience before it became Scripture. . . . The aim of historical exegesis is to read the Old Testament in its various parts in the historical circumstances and conditions of men's minds in which it originated, just that we may trace God's historical fellowship with mankind. . . . Historical exegesis gives us the right idea of Scripture, which is the reflection of the presence of the living God in human history."[1]

The unique inspiration of the Bible will demonstrate itself to all who read it as the narrative of "*God's historical fellowship with mankind,*" and so long as God is found in the history criticism cannot impair its value. To argue that the "higher criticism" destroys our belief in the inspiration of the Old Testament is to contradict the testimony of some of the most accomplished critics. Dr. Driver's clear statement, to which many parallels might be quoted, is : "There is no ground to suppose that, apart from the special illumination vouchsafed to the great teachers who originated or sustained the principles of its faith, the religious history of Israel would have differed materially from that of the kindred nations by which it was surrounded"; and this special illumination he defines as a "unique and extraordinary spiritual insight, enabling them thereby to declare in different degrees and in accordance with the needs or circumstances of particular ages or particular occasions, the mind and purpose of God."[2]

The biblical introduction to the history of humanity is *the narrative of Creation.* "In the beginning God created" is the majestic utterance of a revelation the sublimity of which is enhanced rather than diminished by the discovery of striking parallels to the Old Testament story in traditions current amongst other peoples. The question of the relation of the first two chapters of Genesis to the Babylonian account of Creation is a question of fact which must be decided

[1] *Expositor*, January, 1900.
[2] *Sermons on Subjects connected with the Old Testament*, pp. 137, 146.

by archæologists; from their investigations it appears
that the Babylonian tradition is earlier, although the
Bible story is simpler and purer. But the recognition
of this fact ought not to be prejudicial to faith. To say
that the writer of the account in Genesis derived some
of his materials from Babylonian tradition is neither to
detract from its value as a unique revelation, nor to deprive
it of the authority which rests upon its twofold witness to
the glory of God, who " spake and it was done " (Ps. xxxiii. 9),
and to the glory of man, whom "God created in His own
image" (Gen. i. 27). This view of the origin of the Bible
narrative is inconsistent only with theories of inspiration,
which imply that the purpose of divine revelation is to
impart scientific knowledge and to anticipate modern discoveries. If, on the one hand, such theories are rendered
obsolete, on the other hand we are furnished with a new
and effective reply to those who explain the story in Genesis
as a product of the author's imagination; for on this supposi-
tion the existence amongst other nations of stories which
closely resemble it would be inexplicable. It is arbitrary
to make the inspiration of the writer depend upon the
absolute originality of all the details given in his account,
and to exclude the possibility of his having been guided
in his selection of materials by the divine Spirit. "The
narrative of Genesis i. comes," says Dr. Driver, "at the
end of a long process of gradual elimination of heathen
elements, and of gradual assimilation to the purer teachings of Israelitish theology, carried on under the spiritual
influences of the religion of Israel."

But the Hebrew account of Creation may be described
as a divine revelation, not merely because its author omits

mythological details and all polytheistic elements, but also because his statements about God's creative energy are in striking *contrast* to the words of the great Babylonian epic as translated from the original cuneiform inscriptions :

> Of old, when the heavens above were not named,
> And the earth beneath bore no name,
>
>   .   .   .   .
>
> Of old, when none of the gods existed,
> Then were *the gods* created.

How wide a chasm separates this poetic description of Creation, which includes the gods amongst things that have come to exist, from the simple statement of the eternal truth which Israel learnt from the Creation-narrative, " God was, when all things else began to be." Another noteworthy feature in the Hebrew story of Creation is the statement that God did not form the world out of material already existing. " How," asks Dr. Loofs, " could the great truth that the world had its origin in the free creative will of God be more plainly and intelligibly expressed than in those sublime words, ' God said, Let there be light, and there was light ' ? This twofold element — God's absolute independence of all the world and the origin of the world out of God's creative will—this is the unique element in the biblical narrative of Creation." [1]

It is the religious element in the Hebrew account of Creation which distinguishes it from all other accounts, and imparts to it a supremacy unaffected either by the teachings of modern science or by the results of critical analysis. Geology and astronomy have vastly enlarged our conception of " the world," and have corrected long-

---

[1] *Die Schöpfungsgeschichte*, etc. See *Expository Times*, vol. x. p. 495.

cherished but mistaken interpretations of the story of its
formation, but they have failed to illumine the darkness
which hides the origin of the universe from all who refuse
to say " in the beginning God." The newer criticism has
distinguished the elaborate Elohistic narrative in Genesis
i.–ii. 4*a* from the earlier Jahvistic fragment in Genesis ii.
4*b*–7, but in *both* accounts Creation is described as the work
of God, and man as a being fitted for fellowship human
and divine. Professor Whitehouse—who follows those
critics who distinguish the two Creation narratives, the
earlier being simpler and less abstract in its religious conceptions—says in the closing paragraph of his learned
and luminous article on " Cosmogony " : " The supreme value
of our biblical cosmogony lies in the fact that . . . it sets
God above the great complex world-process, and yet closely
linked with it, as a *personal* intelligence and will that rules
victoriously and without a rival. And as the supreme
object of His creative energy, it sets man, fashioned in His
divine likeness, to be the ruler of created things." How
trivial are the questions around which controversy has
often fiercely raged, as compared with the indisputable fact
that at the threshold of the inspired record there stands
this " clear and sublime attestation of the *personal* source
from which all has flowed, and of the *unique worth and
dignity of man, and his near kinship with that source.*" [1]

The principles which have guided us in our study of the
Creation-narrative apply to the rest of the Old Testament.
Nothing but the study of the Bible itself can teach us in
what its unique inspiration consists ; but the science of

[1] Hastings' *Bible Dictionary*, vol. i. p. 507.

religion will help us to come to right conclusions, if *all* the results of its comparative studies are taken into account, and *the points of contrast* between the Hebrew faith and the heathen religions are as carefully noted as the points of agreement. Modern philosophy teaches us to define the essence of a thing in terms of purpose; as, *e.g.*, the essential qualities of a sermon are not those elements which it possesses in common with other forms of discourse, but those elements which distinguish it from the rest and fit it to accomplish its special purpose. Hence the essential elements of Old Testament inspiration will be discovered not by studying only those features in which it resembles other histories, but by studying also those in which it differs from them, and by the possession of which its claim to be a revelation of the divine Mind must be established.

If the God who wrote the book of Nature is the God who wrote the Bible, it will not surprise us to find in its pages proofs that in the spiritual world God works by methods analogous to those which, according to the teaching of Science, He employs in the evolution of the natural world. Some Old Testament critics have displayed a naturalistic bias; on this account their results should be carefully sifted, but their methods are not of necessity thereby invalidated. It is not easy to estimate our indebtedness to reverent scholars whose patient investigations have cast welcome light upon the historical conditions which determined the growth of the religion of Israel. An advanced critic is not therefore a foe to all that is supernatural; for example, Professor Kittel in the course of his studies is confronted with the fact that Moses' conception of God is distinctly superior to any idea that he could have borrowed from

7

neighbouring tribes; the question, "How did that new and lofty knowledge of God find its way into the soul of Moses?" cannot be evaded; and this is the critic's reply: "When the thought flashed across the mind of Moses that God was neither the world, nor an idealised image of man, but that He was the Lord of life and the author of the moral law . . . that knowledge came neither from his age nor from himself: it came to him from the immediate revelation of this God in his heart." [1]

Spiritual religion has gained much in the past and will gain still more in the future from the researches of historical critics. The determination of the date of a prophetic oracle, or of the chronological order of a narrative, is not merely a matter of literary interest, it has a spiritual value. The words and deeds of Hebrew saints must be viewed in their true historic setting, if their experience is to be understood, and the story of their life and work is to yield " instruction which is in righteousness." But the student who finds in Scripture the record of a development in the purity of moral ideas and in the spirituality of religion should pay special attention to *the highest types of experience*. He will learn most from the patriarchs who had the clearest vision of God and the closest fellowship with Him, and from the prophets who stood nearest to the summit on the ascending pathway that leads through the Old Testament to Christ; for if to one man is given a more spiritual message than another, it is because " the divine personality impresses itself un-equally on different minds." For the same reason some Psalms answer more completely than others to Herder's beautiful description of the Psalter as " the poetry of

[1] *History of the Hebrews*, p. 252.

friendship between the spirit of man and the Spirit of God."

A timely caution was addressed to the first " Science of Religion " Congress held at Stockholm in 1897, by one whose words on this subject have great weight ; Dr. de la Saussaye thinks that there is danger of applying a false standard of value to the materials which are accessible to the student of comparative religion.   Newly discovered documents may be *less* valuable than those with which we have been long familiar, and whilst the lower types of religion should not be ignored, it is of first importance *to understand the higher*.   " The Old Testament and the tragic poets of Greece retain their position, even after we have made the acquaintance of Babylonian formulæ of incantation. . . . The Greeks are Greeks, not by virtue of what they have in common with Australians and Bushmen, but by virtue of that which distinguishes them from such savages, and the value of the Old Testament does not consist in its references to superstitions of which there was even in Israel an abundant growth, but in the higher prophetic faith to which it gives expression." The character of Cromwell has more interest for the scientific student of religion than the misty form of Khuenaten, the reformer-king of the eighteenth Egyptian dynasty.   The various species of fetish - worship which have prevailed amongst negroes and Melanesians ought not to be neglected, but the study of Pascal's *Thoughts* will prove a better preparation for those who desire to understand the true nature of spiritual religion.   Professor de la Saussaye recognises that the theories of the origin of religion advanced by such scholars as Max Müller, Tylor, Vodskov, etc., have

great value as working hypotheses ; " but it is impossible
to accept anyone of these hypotheses to the exclusion of all
the rest, and it is equally impossible to form an eclectic
combination of them." In their own respective spheres
the mythological, the anthropological, the animistic, and
other theories have been of service ; without their aid many
significant facts would never have been discovered, but
they have given no explanation of all the facts, they have
accounted neither for piety nor worship, neither for the
inward nor the outward aspects of true religion. " The great
questions, What is a God ? and Why do men reverence the
gods ? the science of religion does not answer. For an
explanation of the facts we must look elsewhere. Working
hypotheses and theories of the history of religion must not
be accepted as philosophical results." No undervaluing
of the universal features discernible in all religions is implied,
when it is maintained that faith cannot subsist on abstrac-
tions, and that something more than the conviction of God's
immanence in all things is needed to keep faith alive, even
the personal experience of God's present help and salvation.
In brief, the purpose of Dr. de la Saussaye's convincing
argument is to show the insufficiency of all forms of natural
religion, and the living power of historic Christianity.
" Jesus set no limits to the dominion of His Father, but He
fills every moment with an eternal significance by His revelation that the blessedness of personal fellowship with God is
the privilege of every man." [1]

Mr. H. O. Taylor, in the masterly work which well fulfils the
promise of its sub-title, — " a study of intellectual and spiritual
growth from early times to the establishment of Christianity,"

[1] *Die vergleichende Religionsforschung und der religiöse Glaube.*

—has shown that the "Christian thought of God which completed the Hebraic conception of Jehovah, included all elements of verity contained in the lesser thoughts of God and gods held by other peoples"; but he is careful to point out that whilst "Christianity was itself a complete response to all the longings of the time . . . *when its antecedents have been pointed out,* when its scope and the conditions of its rapid spread have been indicated, *its existence is still unaccounted for.* . . . Christianity was a new power in the world, which sprang not altogether from its antecedents, and still less was given birth to by any circumstances of the time. The historian is thus thrown back on the inexplicable personality of Christ." [1]

> Do men dare to call Thy Scripture
>   Mystic forest, unilluminated nook?
> If it be so, O my spirit!
>   Then let Christ arise on thee, and look!
> With the long lane of His sunlight
>   Shall be cut the forest of His book.

[1] *Ancient Ideals,* vol. ii. pp. 401, 234.

Chapter the Seventh

ACCESS TO GOD THROUGH CHRIST

No one knoweth who the Son is, save the Father; and who the
Father is, save the Son, and he to whomsoever the Son willeth to
reveal Him.—LUKE x. 22 (R.V.).

> Surely one star above all souls shall brighten,
>   Leading for ever where the Lord is laid;
> One revelation through all years enlighten
>   Steps of bewilderment, and eyes afraid.
>   —F. W. H. MYERS.

JESUS meets us, as we have already seen, in the domain
of history; scientific students are therefore compelled to
give some account of Him. At this stage of our inquiry
it is of paramount importance that we keep in mind the
distinction it has often been needful to draw between facts
and hypotheses; it is also essential that our investigations
should extend to the facts about Jesus Christ Himself as well
as to the facts about His teaching and His work. Naturalistic views of history, involving the surrender of the
supernatural Christ, are sometimes the result of accepting
conjectures as facts, but more frequently they are the result
of narrowing the range of inquiry so as to exclude the
question, "Who is this Son of man?" (John xii. 34).
It is, however, the great merit of Ritschl and his disciples
that they have forced upon philosophic historians the
question, "What think ye of the Christ?" Too often the

further question, " Whose son is He ? " (Matt. xxii. 42), is shirked ; but *the old dilemma* forces itself upon candid critics, and is reaffirmed from the modern point of view : " either Jesus was a self-deluded fanatic, or He is more than a link in the chain of naturally conditioned human history." Dr. Loofs urges Christians to delineate Jesus with absolute fidelity ; for if this be done, " modern men will be convinced of the impossibility of estimating the person of Jesus on a naturalistic basis. But if at that point in the history of this little earth of ours the Almighty interposed supernaturally in the development of humanity, who shall say that His influence is limited to the sphere of the psychical ? " [1] There is general agreement that amongst the facts of history which have an abiding value for faith a foremost place must be given to the fact of Christ's appearing.

The nineteenth century has restored history to the place of honour from which it had been deposed in the eighteenth century. Harnack has reminded us that Hegel and his great disciple von Ranke have answered the philosophical critics who, like Lessing (1729–81), *looked down upon history* as a strange and ceaseless play of contingent phenomena, arguing that faith cannot rest upon facts which belong to history, and that it is impossible to lay hold upon a single historical appearance and to give to it the weight of eternity. To such teaching Harnack replies in words which are all the more significant because of his sympathy with the advanced criticism of the Gospel narratives : " But the spiritual purport of a whole life, of a personality, is also an historical fact : it has its reality in the effect which

[1] *American Journal of Theology*, July, 1899.

it produces; and it is here that we find the link which binds us to Jesus Christ"; . . . "the main lineaments of Christ's personality and the sense and true point of His sayings have not been altered."[1] Although such a statement leaves the historicity of the resurrection of Christ an open question, it is valuable as the frank confession of a scientific historian that he is confronted by such facts as these: *the personality of Jesus Christ, and the effects which that personality has produced and is producing still.* Noteworthy also is Harnack's more recent and timely utterance in regard to those who so readily find, even in the Synoptic Gospels, reflections of the thought of a later age: "People nowadays, however, put such constructions on the text more readily than is necessary."[2]

Before proceeding further we may recall our definition of religion as "the communion of the soul with God." This communion is "not a monologue, but *a dialogue*," and we have seen how God strives to begin this communion, the purpose of His revelation in Nature and in History being to draw men to seek Him who is not far from each one of us. In communion between man and man the revelation of love is conditional upon the response of trust; it is in the frank interchange of confidences that spirits become known to each other. But the first effect of the consciousness of God's nearness to our spirits is a sense of our distance from Him; moreover, God often speaks to ears that are deaf, and still more frequently to hearts that are dumb. The

[1] *Christianity and History*, pp. 56, 61.

[2] *What is Christianity?* p. 23. For numerous examples of the truth of Harnack's words, see Professor Schmiedel's article on the "Gospels" in the *Encyclopædia Biblica*, vol. ii.

result is that to the consciousness of many seekers it appears
as though their earnest prayers were the beginning of the
communion, whereas their impulse to seek God is a proof
that the Father's search does not end when His voice is
spurned.

Man's first question, as his religious consciousness awakes,
is, " How shall I draw near to God ? " The New Testament
has but one reply to this question, though it is expressed
by different writers with characteristic and instructive
variations : *our access to God is through Christ.* St. Paul
is confident that Christians whom he has never seen have
the same experience as his own converts enjoy : " Now
in Christ Jesus ye that once were far off are made nigh
in the blood of Christ . . . for through Him we both
have our access (τὴν προσαγωγήν) in one Spirit unto the
Father " (Eph. ii. 13, 18, R.V. ; cp. Eph. iii. 12 and Rom.
v. 2). St. Peter is dwelling on the same thought when
he says, " Christ also suffered for sins once, the righteous
for the unrighteous, that He might bring us (προσαγάγῃ)
to God " (1 Pet. iii. 18, R.V.). The writer of the Epistle to
the Hebrews illustrates from the language of the temple and
its priestly ritual the same truth which St. Paul expounds
in its legal aspect : " Having therefore, brethren, boldness
to enter into the holy place by the blood of Jesus, . . .
and having a great priest over the house of God, *let us
draw near* (προσερχώμεθα) with a true heart in fulness of
faith " (Heb. x. 19 ff., R.V.). In view of recent attempts to
contrast the teaching of the apostles with the teaching
of Christ, the words of the Lord Jesus should also be borne
in mind : " No one cometh unto the Father, but by Me "
(John xiv. 6, R.V.) ; " I am the door : by Me if any man

enter in, he shall be saved " (John x. 9). St. Paul's teaching is but the unfolding of the truth contained in germ in these familiar sayings of our Lord ; an admirable critical note on the translation of Romans v. 2 paraphrases the apostle's thought in the words of Christ : " Perhaps both grammar and logic will run in perfect harmony together if we render, ' through Him we have by faith got or obtained our access into this grace wherein we stand.' This rendering will bring to view two causes of getting the access or obtaining the introduction into the state of grace ; one cause *objective*, Christ ; the other *subjective*, faith ; Christ the door, faith the hand that moves the door to open and to admit." [1]

Ritschl and some of his followers recognise no revelation of God either in the beauties of nature or in the moral order of the world. One may admire their anxiety to maintain the supremacy of Christ without assenting to their *disparagement of less complete revelations* of the divine mind and will ; the teachings of history may supplement the teachings of nature, whilst both are preparatory to the final revelation of God in Christ. In many portions and in many modes God spake unto the fathers in the prophets,— the revelation was imparted " piecemeal," and was " multiform,"—but " at the end of these days " He " hath spoken unto us in *His* Son " (Heb. i. 2, R.V.). Herrmann, therefore, does well to remind us that neither thinking of the idea of the Eternal, nor the holding of orthodox beliefs about God, can raise us into the realm of true communion with God ; and we shall do well to instruct men to seek Him, not as the Creator of the world, nor as the Ruler of the ages, but as the God

[1] Canon Evans in *Expositor*, 2nd Series, vol. iii. p. 169.

and Father of our Lord Jesus Christ. A Methodist reader may confess to having felt his heart "strangely warmed" by some of Herrmann's earnest words in his treatise *The Communion of the Christian with God*. At the outset one is struck by his choosing for "communion" a strong word (*Verkehr*), unusual in this connexion, and intended no doubt to express the idea of confidential, intimate intercourse. To one who has sat at the feet of John Wesley it is familiar truth that the only faith worthy of the name is an attitude of the soul, and that such faith alone can determine our relation to God. But the crucial question is, "How does God's revelation of Himself in Christ elicit from man the faith which is unreserved trust in the forgiving love of God, who will not allow the sinner to perish in his sin ?"

Herrmann's reply is, "God makes Himself known to us as *the Power that is with Jesus.* We are obliged, then, to confess that the existence of Jesus in this world of ours is the fact in which God so touches us as to come into communion with us. . . . But the God we recognise is not only the God of Jesus Christ. He is our own God. This follows from the fact that the Man in whom we grasp with certainty the reality of God stands in the attitude of friendship towards men who feel themselves far removed from God. . . . This *personal attitude of Jesus* assures us that His God is our God ; and it thereby uplifts us into the kingdom of God." [1] Of like import are the words in which Harnack explains how the personality of Christ saves us : "Here we have a life that was lived wholly in the fear of God—resolute,

[1] *The Communion of the Christian with God*, p. 79.

unselfish, pure ; here there glows and flashes a grandeur, a love, which draws us to itself.   Although it was all a continual struggle with the world ; though bit by bit one earthly possession after another fell away, and at last the life itself came to an ignominious end ; yet no soul can avoid the thought that whoso dies thus, dies well : he dies not but lives. . . . He is the firstborn among many brothers ; He is our surety for the reality of a future world.   So it is, then, that God speaks to us through Him." [1]

These ardent words have touched many hearts that had been chilled by less attractive forms of Theism ; it is recognised that in Jesus we have more than a teacher, more than an example ; His appearance amongst men, though not irregular, is unique.   As Dr. Hermann Cremer truly says : " It is a great concession that there are facts which have an abiding value for faith, facts from which a religious power goes forth to later generations.   From this position it ought not to be a great step to the recognition of those facts of history in which God acts for us and with us." [2]   Here the issue is clearly stated ; it may well appear as though from " facts which have an abiding value for faith " to " *facts of history in which God acts for us and with us*," it ought not to be a great step, but

> The little more and how much it is,
> And the little less and what worlds away. [3]

The power which the personality of Jesus still exerts over the hearts of men is not explained when it is said that

---

[1] *Christianity and History*, p. 47 ff.
[2] *Glaube, Schrift und heilige Geschichte*, p. 83 f.
[3] Robert Browning, *By the Fireside*.

in Him the true relation of man to God is realised, and that
in Him the grace and truth of God is perfectly revealed. So
far as the former statement is concerned it is indisputable
that the ideal of spiritual religion is exemplified in Jesus,—
His brethren attain the perfect life when through Him they
come into like spiritual relations with God, for " He was able
to remain always in that state of soul which we count blessed."
But are we necessarily lifted into the realm of communion
with God because we know that the Good had once an
existence in this world of sin ? Are we convinced that
humanity cannot be forsaken of God, since it is clear that
Jesus had found Him ? Well does Herrmann say—though
his words seem to us to suggest another conclusion—" We
feel that He first reveals to us what personal, spiritual life
is, and He makes us feel *how starved and perplexed is our own
inner life*. . . . The man who lets himself be mastered by that
power of personal life that is made manifest in Jesus gains
thereby a new fulness of life and is placed in a new world.
He sees now what he could not see before, namely, that his
own manner of life is wrong, and that what he has made of
himself, alas ! is nothing. Through the strength of Jesus he
is made to acknowledge the reality of an Omnipotence which
gives this Man the victory, and from the friendship of Jesus
for the sinners whom He humbles, he gathers courage to
believe that all these things mean God's love seeking out
him, poor sinner as he is." [1] Christians who hold that
Jesus was " declared to be the Son of God with power, according to the spirit of holiness, by the resurrection of the dead "
(Rom. i. 4, R.V.) may read into these gracious words a meaning
they were not intended to convey ; for we are not to ask the

---

[1] *Communion with God*, p. 90 f.

metaphysical questions : Who is he who has for us the value
of God, so that we may accept his words as divine assur-
ances ? How did he gain his knowledge of God's willing-
ness to pardon sinners ? How came he to have the exclusive
right to lead sinners to God ? To know that Jesus Christ
Himself enjoyed constant and intimate communion with God
is not a sufficient basis for the faith which is the beginning
of spiritual religion in a sinner's heart ; but if *God was in
Christ*, communing with men and striving to draw men
into close fellowship with Himself, then in the light of the
Incarnation and the Resurrection of the Son of God each
word, each deed of Jesus becomes a revelation of the grace
of God which appeared in Him,—then He through whose
death we are reconciled to God and by whose life we are
saved (Rom. v. 10) "lays hold upon us," compelling us to
own that "herein is love," that His great deed of love is
the supreme revelation of the heart of God,—the fact of
history in which God acts both for us and with us,
inasmuch as "He loved us, and sent His Son to be the
propitiation for our sins " (1 John iv. 10).

Herrmann's distinction between "the historical portrait
of Jesus" and "the great *picture of Jesus' inner life*" is
made with the intention of placing spiritual religion upon
a foundation which historical criticism cannot touch. But
the historical portrait of Jesus must be constructed from
the New Testament writings, and, as modern lives of Christ
prove, different artists produce different results. Much
depends on individual judgment as to the trustworthiness
of the evangelists, as, for instance, what value is to be placed
on the "front face" portrait of our Lord in the Fourth

Gospel.[1] Herrmann maintains that the personality of Jesus "never lets the contradictions and imperfections of the story disfigure the clear features of that which it gave to men, namely, Jesus' own inner life." [2] Expression is here given to a truth, not the whole truth assuredly, but a truth which has an important bearing on controversies affecting the fundamentals of faith and arising out of attempts to solve the difficult problem of the literary origin of the Gospels. Why should Herrmann's statement be limited to the inner life of Jesus ? the records of that inner life are no more and no less historic than the narratives of His mighty and gracious deeds, nor are they less exposed to the sifting of critical research. Unless the Christ of history is the living Christ, it is impossible to stifle the sigh :

> Ah ! would my Lord were here amongst us still
>   Proffering His bosom to His servant's brow !
>   Too oft that holy life comes o'er us now
> Like twilight echoes from a distant hill.[3]

Upon the trustworthiness of the evangelists we depend as well for the record of the public words and works of Christ, which also give us glimpses into His inner life, as for the narrative of the Temptation, which embodies the disciples' remembrance of words in which Jesus Himself disclosed secrets of His inner life, which would otherwise never have been known. The appeal to the experience of the Christian

---

[1] Schmiedel describes the Fourth Gospel as "the ripest fruit of primitive Christianity," but the existence of primitive Christianity is inexplicable on the assumption that Christ Himself is a fiction, the imaginative creation of "a great and eminent soul," who in this gospel "gives expression to *his deep ideas* in the form of a life of Jesus." See *Encyclopædia Biblica*, vol. ii. p. 2554.

[2] *Communion with God*, p. 63.   [3] Charles Tennyson Turner,

—to " the portrait of Jesus which he carries within him "—
is a legitimate appeal, and when historical criticism of the
New Testament writings has been allowed " full play," the
portrait within will be found in all essential features to
resemble the picture of the personality of Jesus as it is
painted in the Gospels.

How delicate are some of the questions involved in
present-day criticism of the Gospels is evident from the
difficulty experienced by so courageous and devout a scholar
as Dr. Sanday in the interpretation of St. Matthew's statement (iii. 2) that John the Baptist came " saying, Repent
ye ; *for the kingdom of heaven is at hand*." The note on this
verse is, " Stress can hardly be laid on the form of announcement in Matt. iii. 2, which would make the Baptist anticipate exactly the announcement of Jesus. This would seem
to be due to the editor. The oldest version describes the
Baptist as ' preaching a baptism of *repentance* for remission
of sins ' (Mark i. 4)." But in a later passage Dr. Sanday
says : " The announcement which they (the Twelve) were
to make by word of mouth was limited to the one formula
with which *both John and Jesus* had begun, ' The kingdom
of heaven is at hand ' (Matt. x. 7). . . . John, Jesus Himself,
and the apostles all opened their ministry with the same
announcement." Here the second thought is probably
better than the first ; but the earlier note is the suggestion
of a reverent critic, and lends additional weight to his own
careful conclusion : " Even if we make to negative criticism
larger concessions than we have any right to make, there
will still remain in the Gospel picture ineffaceable features
which presuppose and demand that estimate of the Person

of Christ which we can alone call in the strict sense Christian." [1]

The supposed opposition between the Christ of experience and the Christ of the Gospels is to a large extent the result of an exaggerated estimate of the negative results of historical criticism. *The appeal to experience* confirms the accuracy of the evangelists' portrait not only of the inner life of Jesus, but also of the whole personality of Him, whose "words" proved that He was "in the Father," and whose "works" proved that the Father was in Him (John xiv. 10). Moreover, the inner life of Jesus is revealed both in His teaching which bears witness to the intimacy of His communion with the Father, and in His gracious deeds which are the sign that the Father was abiding in Him. [2]

Modern discussions of Christology have made us familiar with another assumed opposition,—*the historic Jesus and the exalted Christ* are set over against each other in vivid contrast, as though the risen Lord in whom we trust were of necessity the creation of some metaphysical theologian, and as though "the name which is above every name" could not possibly be the name of Jesus, who "humbled Himself, becoming obedient even unto death, yea, the death of the cross" (Phil. ii. 8, 9, R.V.). But the appeal to experience does not confirm the alleged lack of harmony between the Son of man who was the friend of publicans and sinners

[1] Hastings' *Dictionary of the Bible*, vol. ii. pp. 610, 614, 648.
[2] Cp. F. D. Maurice's words: "I rise gradually to believe, not on the authority of any Samaritan woman or Church doctor, but because I have heard Christ for myself, speaking to me *out of His book*, and speaking to me *in my heart*, and therefore know that He is indeed the Saviour who should come into the world."

8

and the Son of man who is now at the right hand of God. Have not His twentieth-century disciples truer knowledge of Him than the men who were His companions throughout His earthly ministry? They heard Him teach and they heard Him pray, they saw Him heal the sick and raise the dead, but

> They asked the very Way, Where lies the Way?
> The very Son, Where is the Father's face?[1]

Was it not faith in the risen Jesus which led these men who were " slow of heart to believe " to collect those precious reminiscences of His earthly life without which there would have been no portrait of the historic Jesus? How frankly they record the Master's question, " Do ye not yet understand ? " (Mark viii. 21, R.V.), and His charge, when they knew not what the rising from the dead should mean, that " they should tell no man what things they had seen, save when the Son of man should have risen again from the dead " (Mark ix. 9, R.V.). These sayings of Jesus, taken from the Gospel which probably represents the earliest and most direct tradition, imply what is distinctly stated by St. John that only in the light of Christ's resurrection did His hard sayings become plain: " When therefore He was raised from the dead, His disciples remembered that He spake this ; and they believed the scripture, and the word which Jesus had said " (John ii. 22, R.V.).

It is true that the Gospel *of* Jesus—by which is meant our knowledge of His own spiritual life—can be distinguished from the Gospel *about* Jesus—by which is meant the glad tidings of salvation through faith in His name. But if the

[1] Dr. George Macdonald.

appeal be made to *the experience of the early Christians*, there can be no doubt that faith in Christ was the heart's response to the apostles' preaching as they " witnessed of God that He raised up Christ." " So we preach, and so ye believed " (1 Cor. xv. 11) is an appeal to the Corinthians' experience of the saving power of the gospel as well as to their remembrance of the " glad tidings " that Paul proclaimed. With freshness and force this argument has recently been stated : " It is certain that Christianity had birth in the intense belief of the apostolic circle that Christ was risen from the dead. . . . Either the belief sprang from the only fact which accounts for it—a fact transcending scientific treatment—or this fact never occurred, we have no explanation of apostolic belief, and again scientific treatment is excluded. As in the uncritical centuries which are past, so now, after subjection to criticism, the records of the life of Christ present enough sure fact to make His personality as deep a mystery as the apostolic belief in His resurrection." [1]

Thus in modern discussions an ancient dilemma finds expression in this form : *denial of the resurrection of Christ intensifies rather than relieves the mystery of His personality* ; moreover, it leaves the experience of the early Christians unexplained. Nor should it be forgotten that no later witness can have such weight as theirs ; many of these disciples retained a vivid remembrance of the historic Jesus and of the risen Saviour ; they had also present communion with the living Christ (cp. 1 Cor. xv. 6). When we say that Christians who live in " the dispensation of the Spirit " know Christ better than the men and women who walked and talked with Him on earth, obviously the statement does

---

[1] Taylor, *Ancient Ideals*, vol. ii. p. 233.

not include those who waited for "the promise of the Father" and to whom the descent of the Spirit was the proof that Jesus had ascended to the right hand of God. The early Christians did not say, as they spoke of Christ's sufferings and death, "Whoso dies thus, dies well; he dies not, but lives." Their gospel was, "He was delivered up for our trespasses, and was raised for our justification" (Rom. iv. 25, R.V.). The sufferings of Christ they now saw in the transfiguring light of the glory which shone upon the historic cross when God raised Jesus from the dead; the words of Christ they now read with deeper insight into the infinite significance of the historic teaching; the gentleness of Christ they now recalled with new reverence for the divine majesty of the historic Person, whose self-witness "I am meek and lowly in heart" suggests no doubt of His humility, and whose promise, "Come unto Me, all ye that labour and are heavy laden, and I will give you rest" (Matt. xi. 28), suggests no doubt of His power. The historic Christ was not less to them but more, as they compared the portrait of Jesus graven on their memories with the image of Christ that was being formed in their hearts (Gal. iv. 19). In one significant passage even Herrmann seems to grant this: "Whenever the person of Jesus touches us as a fact that is real to ourselves, then we hear the gospel preached. Not everyone, indeed, can see the personal life of Jesus. We see it only when it pleases God to reveal His Son in us."[1] Between the Christ of the Gospels and the Christ of the Epistles there is in the Christian consciousness no contradiction, nor even discord. It is impossible to know too well the Christ of the Gospels; the more accurate is our know-

[1] *Communion with God*, p. 68.

ledge of Him, the clearer will be our vision of the exalted
Christ who is the same Jesus.   But to-day it is of chief
importance to dwell upon the truth that " the history (of
Jesus Christ) as a whole, and His death in particular, must
be conceived from the point of view of the apostle who
exhibits to us the exalted Christ as the key to the understanding of His history, if our faith in Him is to be the faith
of the apostle, that is, if Christ is to be to us the power of
God for our redemption from sin and death." [1]

The key-stone of the arch which supports the Christian
faith, and which rests on the one side upon the argument
from history, and on the other side upon the argument
from experience, is *the Resurrection of Jesus*.   This unique
fact connects the Gospels with the Epistles, and it belongs
to two realms of truth ; it is a fact of history to which facts
of Christian experience also bear witness.   The scientific
historian sifts the objective evidence and declares its value,
whilst the Christian believer finds the subjective evidence
a ground of personal certainty and convinces others of its
value as he walks in " newness of life."   In this respect the
evidence for Christ's resurrection is superior to the evidence
for His miracles.   " We can accept a phenomenon as supernatural," says Dr. Loofs, " only when we have cogent reasons
for so doing.   Thus one may experience the ' power of the
resurrection of Christ ' (Phil. iii. 10).   No such inner cor-
roboration is possible for any of the other miracles narrated
of Jesus." [2]   That belief in the resurrection of Jesus makes
the miraculous stories of the Gospels more credible is an

[1] Somerville, *St. Paul's Conception of Christ*, p. 237.
[2] *American Journal of Theology*, July, 1899.

inference which Dr. Loofs would not accept; he is careful to claim for the scientific conscience its full rights in the criticism of the Gospel narratives. If, however, the living Christ whom we know as the Christ of experience is the Christ who died and rose again, it is clear that doubts as to the credibility of this or that " incidental " miracle[1] do not touch the " essential " miracle which is sufficiently attested as an objective fact, abundantly verified in the subjective sphere by the experience of successive generations of Christians, and which, therefore, abides as the foundation fact of the Christian religion.

The inward certainty which comes from experience of the power of Christ's resurrection does not make the believer indifferent to the results of historical inquiry into the trustworthiness of the facts of the Gospel history; on the other hand, objections to the credibility of the narratives based on variations in the evangelists' accounts of the appearances of the risen Saviour cannot shake the faith of him who has been raised with Christ from the death of sin and is " alive unto God in Christ Jesus " (Rom. vi. 11, R.V.).

---

[1] According to Professor Schmiedel " the foundation pillars for a truly scientific life of Jesus" are His compassion and His preaching. But no scientific reason is given for the rejection of those Gospel narratives which do not accord with the critic's assumption that " the divine is to be sought in Jesus only in the form in which it is capable of being found in a man." Schmiedel's attempt to explain away the account of the resurrection of Lazarus may serve to show that this so-called scientific life of Jesus is not based on facts but on fictions. " The story is a development of the parable of Lazarus in Luke xvi. 19-31. . . . We can *imagine* that some preacher after relating that parable, in order to open it up to his hearers, *may have added* the remark, ' This Lazarus actually did rise from the dead.' A hearer of this sermon—*so let us further suppose*—gave the notes of it in a shorter form to a third person, who *gathered from it* as a statement of historical fact that Lazarus had risen."—*Encyclopædia Biblica*, vol. ii. p. 2539.

The combination of *internal and external evidence* of the reality of Christ's resurrection proves that the distinction between subjective and objective truth is not absolute ; so far from the one being independent of the other, " the power that worketh in us " is the manifestation and attestation of the " working of the strength of His might, which," according to historic tradition, " He wrought in Christ, when He raised Him from the dead, and made Him to sit at His right hand in the heavenly places " (Eph. iii. 20, i. 19 f., R.V.).

The true way of returning to Christ, as Dr. Drummond teaches in his thorough investigation of " the relation of the apostolic teaching to the teaching of Christ," is not to try to get behind the apostles to Christ Himself, but to study *both the Gospels and the Epistles*, remembering that " the Spirit that taught the apostles is with us still. But we can never dispense with them. . . . We do them an injustice if we exalt them above Christ. We do them as great injustice when we forget that without them we could have had no certainty of the mind of Christ." [1] An historical argument of considerable weight is advanced in these able lectures : in point of time the Gospels appeared *midway* between the Epistles of St. Paul and the Epistles of St. John, and yet " Paul's view, the earliest recorded view of the person of Christ, is very little different from the latest, that of John." Harnack, indeed, says that in *John's* Gospel " we have portrayed . . . a speaking, acting *Pauline* Christ." It is impossible, therefore, to trace a development in the view of the person of Christ from the Synoptic Gospels through Paul to John, for the Gospels appear in the midst of the lofty flights of contemplation

[1] The Kerr Lectures for 1900, p. 411 f. ; cp. p. 219.

which are characteristic of both the Pauline and Johannine writings, and " the conclusion one arrives at is that it is not the fundamental conception that varies, but the type of mind that presents it."

Our inquiry into the facts recorded in the New Testament has shown that according to the apostles' interpretation of the historic fact of Christ's appearing and of their own fellowship with the living Lord, Jesus "lays hold on" sinners, not because He lived in communion with God, but because He who " was dead " is " alive for evermore " (Rev. i. 18), and "ever liveth to make intercession for them " (Heb. vii. 25). Hence the argument of this chapter—in which we have endeavoured to show that our access to God is through Christ, because God was in Christ—reaches its climax in the truth which is unfolded in the Epistle to the Hebrews. The claim of Christianity to be the final religion is in that Epistle based upon the fact that it extends to every believer the privilege of *free access to God through Christ* ; but it is the contemplation of the priestly service of the ascended Christ that emboldens the writer to speak of " a better hope, through which we draw nigh unto God " (vii. 19, R.V.). These words contain what Dr. A. B. Bruce truly calls " the dogmatic centre of the Epistle ; setting forth Christianity as the religion of the better hope by comparison with the earlier religion ; absolutely as the religion of good hope, because the religion through which men for the first time enter into intimate fellowship with God " ; moreover, the final exhortation of the Epistle (x. 19 ff.) " rests on and is expressed in terms of the central truth. Christ has made it possible to have *perfect fellowship with God* ; that is the objective significance of the Christian era. Therefore, draw near, realise your privilege subjectively." [1]

But the writer, who gazes so intently on the Son of God in His exaltation, and directs our thoughts so earnestly to the eternal Priest who has entered the Holy Place, is familiar with details of the life of the historic Jesus. How frequently and with what emphasis he employs the human name *Jesus* ; how confidently he appeals to the trials and temptations of Jesus " in the days of His flesh " (ii. 18, v. 7), in order that upon facts and not upon theories he may base his proof of the sympathy of the great High-priest, who by life's discipline was perfectly fitted to be " a priest for ever " ; how completely he removes the barrier which sin had raised between man and God by reminding his readers of that historic deed, when He who now appears before the face of God for us " put away sin by the sacrifice of Himself " (ix. 26).

As to the relation of these truths to the teaching of Christ, Dr. Drummond truly says that in the intercessory prayer of our Lord (John xvii.) " we have something from His own lips more than sufficient to justify all that the writer of the Epistle to the Hebrews has said. What he has done has been simply to lay hold on the living, exalted Christ within the veil, and in the vivid light of these prayers of the days of His flesh, the tragedy of His death, and the triumph of His resurrection, show men that what He did then He does still. His death remains the permanent plea of the living Christ on behalf of every soul that comes unto God by Him." [2] Readers of the Epistle to the Hebrews

---

[1] *Expositor*, 3rd Series, vol. x. p. 197 ; 4th Series, vol. ii. p. 131.

[2] *Op. cit.* p. 299.

with its advanced Christology do not lose the historic Jesus ; they have no need of the exhortation, " Back to the Christ of the Gospels," for the Jesus, whom this Epistle portrays in His glory, exhibits the traits which were conspicuous in His earthly life ; He is " the same yesterday and to-day, yea and for ever " (xiii. 8, R.V.) ; therefore, He is now " touched with the feeling of our infirmities " (iv. 15). Those who look away from earth to " the Author and Perfecter of faith . . . who hath sat down at the right hand of the throne of God," find that He on whom they gaze is none other than " Jesus . . . who for the joy that was set before Him endured the cross, despising shame " (xii. 2). The great cloud of witnesses is composed " of them that have faith unto the saving of the soul " (x. 39); and although in this Epistle the work of the Holy Spirit in the heart of man is not prominent, its author knows that those who by the blood of Jesus draw near to God have responded to the influences of " *the Spirit of grace* " (x. 29), in whom we have through Christ our access unto the Father.

Chapter the Eighth

ACCESS TO GOD IN THE SPIRIT

But if any man hath not the Spirit of Christ, he is none of His.
—Rom. viii. 9. (R.V.).

> Whoso has felt the Spirit of the Highest
> Cannot confound nor doubt Him nor deny:
> Yea, with one voice, O world, tho' thou deniest,
> Stand thou on that side, for on this am I.
> —F. W. H. Myers.

In his *Aids to Reflection* (1825) Coleridge makes suggestive reference to the prejudice which had been aroused by Methodist teaching in regard to the work of the Holy Spirit: "Before you give way to the emotions of distaste or ridicule, reflect again and again, and be sure you understand the doctrine before you determine on rejecting it; if you have resolved that all belief of a divine Comforter present to our inmost being and aiding our infirmities is forced and fanatical; if the Scriptures promising and asserting such communion are to be explained away, in what better light can prayer appear to you than the groans of a wounded lion in his solitary den, or the howl of a dog with his eyes on the moon?" These words, written three-quarters of a century ago, have gained rather than lost in force and fitness. That the Holy Spirit helps the infirmities of the human spirit is a truth vital to spiritual religion, and the effect of philosophic thought in recent years has been to give this truth new prominence. Deeper study of the facts of human consciousness has shown that what the Scripture describes as the indwelling of the Spirit of God is essential to true self-realisation, and therefore essential to communion with God.

Reasonable men will not reject the testimony of the Christian consciousness until, as Coleridge says, they can state the grounds on which they hold that it is the experience of fanatics; especially will they pause, when they find that *the promises of Scripture and the witness of believers agree.* On such a subject the appeal must necessarily be to experience, but the argument from experience is misused when it is so stated as to imply that other forms of evidence are needless. John Wesley often appealed to experience, but, as will hereafter be shown, he never based his arguments upon experience alone. St. Paul, too, made frequent and instructive use of the argument from experience, but he placed it alongside of others; sometimes he connects the inward certainty with the familiar appeal in which there is a ring of triumph: "for what saith the scripture?" (Rom. iv. 3); sometimes he connects the inward certainty with the historic deed which is its basis, as when he says to Christians who have " believed " and " are saved," " If Christ hath not been raised, your faith is vain; ye are yet in your sins " (1 Cor. xv. 17, R.V.); sometimes he connects the inward certainty with the actual results which are manifest in the outward life, as when he points to the appearance of " the fruit of the Spirit " as evidence that the Spirit has been received (Gal. v. 22; cp. iii. 2). The argument from experience is not discredited by the charge that it depends upon an appeal to feelings. This is not its sole basis; more-over, feelings are facts which must be accounted for and which may be subjected to tests. The believer who has "felt" may by thought and inquiry establish the credi-bility of the facts which prove that his faith accords with reason.

In the presence of doubt Tennyson "arose and answered, I have felt," and "*that* is mysticism," says Mr. Andrew Lang. If so, Coleridge was a mystic, for those moving words about the "divine Comforter" rise from the heart of one whose intellect rejected the doctrine of the Divinity of Christ, but whose spiritual needs Unitarianism could not satisfy. After describing Socinianism as " moonlight " and Methodism as a " stove," he exclaims, " Oh for some power to unite heat and light! " There is sufficient truth in this antithesis to make it suggestive of thought; but neither in the intellectual nor in the spiritual life are heat and light—emotion and knowledge—contradictories which mutually exclude each other. Emotions do not arise apart from knowledge, and in every act of knowledge there is some feeling of interest, however slight. But as the two terms are commonly under-stood, there is as great danger of knowledge despising emotion as of emotion being content with ignorance. Men of light and leading need to watch carefully lest the flame of holy fervour should burn low, whilst disciples who are " foolish " soon discover that the sacred fire glows more brightly in the heart when the Lord opens the mind to understand the Scriptures (Luke xxiv. 32, 45). In spiritual experience the emotion which spurs the will to action is roused by the knowledge which enlightens the conscience ; the testimony of the Christian consciousness in regard to *the relation of knowledge to feeling* in the spiritual life is that neither can say to the other, " I have no need of thee."   In the seven-fold gifts of the Spirit all that can minister to the increase of enlightenment as well as to the intensifying of zeal is comprised ; He " lightens with celestial fire," and His

> blessed unction from above
> Is comfort, life, and fire of love.

The experience of the early Christians yields abundant proof that in *the communion of the Holy Spirit* believers drew near to the Father through the Son.   By His Spirit the risen Christ was in contact with their spirits, and the outpouring of the Spirit in their hearts was rightly regarded as the outpouring of the *Father's* love (cp. Isa. xliv. 3 ; Rom. v. 5).   This is the substance of the apostolic experi-ence ; but the same thought finds expression in the words of the Lord Jesus : when He said " the Spirit of Truth . . . shall be in you," He explained the promise as implying His own coming ; and the assurance " I come unto you " He explained as implying the coming of the Father,—" *we* will come and make our abode " with those who love Me and keep My word (cp. John xiv. 17–23).   On the other hand, in passages where the thought rapidly and almost imperceptibly passes from the human spirit to the divine Spirit there is never any infringement upon the distinctness of the human and divine personalities.   The spirit ($\pi\nu\epsilon\hat{\upsilon}\mu\alpha$) is " essenti-ally that part of the man which holds communion with God," and when St. Paul says, " ye are . . . *in the spirit,* if so be that *the Spirit of God dwelleth in you* " (Rom. viii. 9, R.V.), he naturally passes " from thinking of the way in which the $\pi\nu\epsilon\hat{\upsilon}\mu\alpha$ in its best moods acts upon the character . . . to that

influence from without which keeps it in its best moods";
yet even here, closely linked as the Spirit of God is with the
spirit of man in the mind of the apostle and in the experience which he is describing, "the very ease with which
St. Paul changes and inverts his metaphors shows that the
divine immanence with him nowhere means Buddhistic or
Pantheistic absorption." [1]

Such aspects of truth must not be neglected through fear
of their being denounced as mystical. The false Mysticism
must be distinguished from the true. The mysticism of
St. Paul and St. John, which may be traced to the teaching
of Christ, is a perpetual witness to the higher possibilities
of the spiritual life, and an ever-sounding call to Christians
to press forward to their realisation; and as regards false
forms of Mysticism, they are most effectually exposed by
an experimental acquaintance with the New Testament
doctrine of the Holy Spirit.

> God's voice is of the heart,—I do not say
> All voices of the heart, therefore, are God's;
> And to discern the voice amidst the voices
> Is that hard task that we are born to. [2]

The safeguard against the false Mysticism which would
promote spiritual religion by maltreating the body is to be
found in the Pauline doctrine that the body is "a temple
of the Holy Spirit" (1 Cor. vi. 19, R.V.). *The ascetic ideal
of religion* is probably not in the ascendant to-day, when
the gospel of physical culture is so earnestly preached; but
occasionally such a sentence as "Tennyson failed to appreciate
spiritual and ascetic religion" betrays a tendency thus
to limit the meaning of spiritual religion. There is, how-

---

[1] Sanday and Headlam, *Int. Crit. Comm. in loco.*   [2] A. H. Clough.

ever, nothing in true Mysticism to encourage that " severity
to the body" which St. Paul condemned, because it was
" not of any value against the indulgence of the flesh" (Col.
ii. 23, R.V.).   "Christian Mysticism" as the Bampton
Lecturer on this subject has well said, "enjoins a dying life,
not a living death" (cp. Col. iii. 3–6).   The enemy of the Spirit
is not the body, but the flesh [1] with its affections and lusts ;
hence the Christian whilst in the body is not to be under the
dominion of the flesh ; on the contrary, the spirit is to rule
the body and to use its members in the service of holiness
—a result which St. Paul regards as following from the permanent indwelling of the Holy Spirit (cp. Rom. viii. 9).
The due honouring of the body, therefore, means not only
that the body is no longer an armoury, wherein evil passions
find weapons with which to do their deadly work, but
that the members of the body—tongue and eye, and hand
and foot—are weapons at the disposal of their rightful
Lord, to use, as seems best to Him, in the warfare against
sin (cp. Rom. vi. 13, R.V. margin).   And inasmuch as
on the body such honour has been conferred that its
members in obedience to the Spirit may serve the divine
will, it follows that neither by prodigal dissipation of physical
strength nor by neglect of bodily exercise must the intellect
be enfeebled, the affections dulled, or the will paralysed,
lest the spirit be rendered unfit for the higher life of thought
and will and action to which in "the communion of the
Holy Spirit" it may attain.   So dependent on bodily conditions is the efficiency of the various powers of the human

---

[1] See Rom. viii. 4 ff., 1 Cor. iii. 1 ff., where, as in other passages in
St. Paul's Epistles, "flesh" refers to "the principle of sin and its seat
in man's fallen nature," whilst "spirit" refers to "the principle of the
regenerate or divine life in man."

spirit in which the divine Spirit dwells, that the answer to the prayer,

> Lord, arm me with Thy Spirit's might,

is conditional upon the reality of the consecration, which finds fitting expression in an earlier verse of the hymn :

> *Thou hast my flesh*, Thy hallowed shrine,
> Devoted solely to Thy will.

False Mysticism strives after *the absorption of self in God* ; but true Mysticism, so far from involving the suppression of self, implies the enriching of self,—the unfolding and perfecting of all the powers of the human spirit. The analysis of personality in an earlier chapter may be here recalled, for, according to the teaching of Christ and the apostles, the Holy Spirit is a person. When, therefore, we speak of " the communion of the Spirit," we mean that the spiritual nature of man may be influenced by the divine Spirit in all ways in which it is possible for one person to influence another. But there is an element of mysticism in all spiritual fellowship, whether the persons who hold intercourse are human or divine :

> We are spirits clad in veils,
> Man by Man was never seen ;
> All our deep communing fails
> To remove the shadowy screen.

This experience is not peculiar to the spiritual life ; nevertheless, we know that our influence upon each other is real, although our knowledge of each other is imperfect. " Iron sharpeneth iron ; so a man sharpeneth the countenance of his friend " (Prov. xxvii. 17): a man's face will testify to the character of the company he keeps and to the nature of the influences which mould his inner life. It

9

is, therefore, in accordance with this analogy, when Scripture explains the experience of the saints as the effect of the Holy Spirit's influences on the human personality in the respective spheres of thought, emotion, and volition ; and the uniform witness of the Christian consciousness is that in the spirit-filled personality the mind is enlightened and guided, the affections are purified and deepened, the will is strengthened and controlled.   Never is a man so certain that he is of free-will putting forth his own spiritual energy as when he is conscious that the Holy Spirit has imparted to him the desire and the strength to say " I will."

> Let all my powers Thine entrance feel,

is the believer's prayer in one of the Wesleys' noble Hymns to the Holy Spirit, in which are the mystical lines :

> Plunged in the Godhead's deepest sea,
> And lost in Thine immensity.

If " the communion of the Spirit " is a reality, St. Paul teaches that its results will be manifest in the humility and unison of Christians' *thoughts*, in the harmony of their *affections*, and in the absence of party-feeling and self-seeking from the motives which influence the *will* (Phil. ii. 1–4).

The true Mysticism, which is inseparable from the teaching of the New Testament in regard to the work of the Holy Spirit in the hearts of believers, cannot be charged with neglecting any of the elements of spiritual religion. The history of the Church is a record of the thoughts and actions of men who have been guided and energised by the Holy Spirit.   When Herrmann accuses Mysticism

of producing " intellectual dreamers—mere visionaries,"
or " glib talkers about their feelings,—people who in their
ecstatic joy in the Eternal forget temporal affairs and
forget themselves," [1] he is not describing the effects of
true Mysticism. Spiritual religion consists neither in
intellectual contemplation nor in excited emotions, though
thoughts and feelings may alike be the media by which
the Holy Spirit strives with man in order to persuade him
to yield his will to God. Sometimes He brings to remembrance the Saviour's words, learnt in childhood, and lying,
as psychologists would say, beneath the threshold of consciousness ; sometimes He stirs the emotions by setting
Christ crucified before the eyes of the heart; sometimes
He pricks the conscience by His stern witness to some
secret sin. But whether He convict by reasoning of sin, of
righteousness, and of judgment, or melt the heart to con-
trition by thoughts of the Saviour's love, His appeal is to
the entire personality ; and the response for which He longs
is not the self-annihilation of the mystic, but the self-surrender which is a conscious act,—the glad volition of a
soul that consents to feel the conquering love of God.

Christians need to be reminded that " devotions " which
are nothing but stimulus and enjoyment are morally ener-
vating. " The way to God lies through the conscience " ;
in true communion he who quietly listens to the " still
and small and inward voice " gains a clearer sense of duty,
and contemplation issues in action. It is impossible to
insist too earnestly on *the necessity for the activity of every
power of the human spirit* in every act of communion with
God. The fading leaves reminded the prophet of the need

[1] *Warum bedarf unser Glaube geschichtlicher Thatsachen*, p. 22.

for spiritual energy, if the soul is not to lose its grasp of God. "We all do fade as a leaf; and our iniquities, like the wind, take us away"; a feeble hold of the tree of life is the inevitable result of neglecting prayer, "there is none that calleth upon Thy name, that *stirreth up himself to take hold of Thee*" (Isa. lxiv. 6, 7, R.V.). Herrmann's denunciations of spiritual reverie would be far more helpful than they are, if his recognition of the need for diligent exertion of human powers were accompanied by a recognition of man's need of the Spirit who "maketh intercession for the saints according to the will of God" (Rom. viii. 27). The prayer that availeth much is not the product of the unassisted powers of man, however energetically they may be used; it is the supplication of one who has been "strengthened with power through His Spirit in the inward man" (Eph. iii. 16, R.V.). Because the way to God lies through the conscience, our guilty fears must be dispelled by the Spirit of Adoption, who cries Abba, Father, in our hearts (Gal. iv. 6). As "men of flesh and blood" we enter into the chamber to pray to our Father in heaven, but there we must be led by the Spirit and walk by the Spirit, or we shall fulfil the lust of the flesh (Gal. v. 16). When at the hour of communion "we know not how to pray as we ought," the willing spirit is enabled to triumph over the weakness of the flesh by the remembrance of the truth that the Searcher of hearts knows the mind of the Spirit who "maketh intercession for us" (Rom. viii. 26).

Another characteristic of true Mysticism is that it never claims to have access to the Father in the Spirit except *through the Son*. Ritschl's inadequate treatment of the work of the Holy Spirit, as Mr. Garvie rightly remarks, may to some extent be explained by " the limited range of his religious experience "; the same writer has also done good service by bringing before English readers extracts from the writings of Ritschlians who have striven to supply the defects in their master's teaching. To Mr. Garvie's work we are indebted for the following instructive quotation from Kaftan, who clearly states an important truth : " The Spirit of God, which illumines, is the Spirit of the Lord, and the enlightenment is according to its content nothing else than the saving knowledge of Jesus Christ, that is, not of a principle, which He brought into the world, but of His historical person. If, accordingly, these two moments coincide, the perfect knowledge of Jesus Christ and the enlightenment by the Spirit of God, then indeed they are logically related to one another in such a way that the enlightenment springs out of the knowledge of Jesus Christ, not in the reverse way, that a man might have in the enlightenment of the Holy Spirit, which might occur inde· pendently of Christ, the principle of the knowledge of Christ."[1]

True Mysticism, whilst giving the Holy Spirit due honour in the work of human salvation, still seeks to know the Father only as He is revealed in the Son. He who said, " *I glorified Thee* on the earth, having accomplished the work which Thou hast given Me to do " (John xvii. 4, R.V.), said of " the Spirit of truth " who was afterwards to come, " *He shall glorify Me* " (John xvi. 14). As Jesus glorified the Father by accomplishing His redeeming work, so the Holy Spirit glorifies the Son by administering His finished work. The Methodist doctrine of the " direct witness of the

[1] *The Ritschlian Theology*, p. 387 ff.

Spirit " is not exposed to the danger which Kaftan so greatly fears, and against which he so energetically protests ; it certainly does not represent the work of the Holy Spirit as transcending or superseding the perfect revelation of Christ. " Our doctrine," as Dr. Pope expounds it, " is the direct witness of the Spirit, *as alone having in His power the things of Christ* " ; and then in words which wisely guard us against extremes on this subject, the revered teacher, who has helped many to see in the mystical aspects of truth glimpses into the deep things of God, says of some whose " ambition is to hold direct communion with God : they seek, as it were, prematurely to behold Him face to face ; they rise above all subordinate means ; even the Bible is beneath their feet ; Jacob's ladder between heaven and earth is not ethereal enough for them. Hence their assurance is always liable to the penalty of presumption. The inward light may sometimes thus arise in the soul ; but that is not the ordinary manner of the Lord God with man. Our teaching sends sinners to the Spirit, with the cry on their lips, ' We would see Jesus ! ' whose Person and work are the foundation of the word of promise, upon which faith, inwrought of the Holy Ghost, lays hold." [1]

If, however, a false Mysticism may lead to the undervaluing of God's revelation in Christ, a false Naturalism may lead to *the undervaluing of the work of the Holy Spirit*, who reveals the Son. How admirably is this truth expressed in the Rev. W. M. Bunting's hymn :

> Thou gav'st the word, and must apply ;
> Thou know'st the Son, and must make known ;

---

[1] *The Peculiarities of Methodist Doctrine*, p. 13.

> In vain He died, and rose on high,
>   And stoops beseeching from His throne,
> *Till Thou this alien heart prepare*
> *And gain for Christ an entrance there.*

In the discussions to which German theologians have been roused by the rapid spread of Ritschl's teachings, nothing is more noticeable than the identification of Methodist doctrine with the pietistic and mystical views to which most Ritschlians are so strongly opposed. By orthodox Lutheran opponents of this modern school of thought it is regarded as an excellent feature of a system which in the main they condemn, that " it opposes the subjective piety of many circles, the tendency of which is to a methodistico-pietistic undervaluing of the objective factors of Christianity." [1] Another writer, whose object is to show that religion does not consist in pious feelings and experiences, extols Ritschl for his " antagonism to a Methodistic and subjective Pietism." [2]

These writers appear to be ignorant of the fact that Wesley has by anticipation met this objection in his controversial writings, where as severely as Ritschl or Herrmann he condemns such " undervaluing of the objective factors of Christianity " as marred the spiritual teaching of the Moravians. That the communion of the Holy Spirit is a privilege of Christian experience he consistently maintained, and if that be Mysticism he would have gloried in the name. " I pretend to the Spirit just so far as is essential to a state of salvation," he says in the letter in which he declares that he could name persons " at London, at Bristol, at Kingswood, at Newcastle," whose changed lives were a sufficient answer

---

[1] Haack, *Ueber den fundamentalen Unterschied der Ritschlschen und der kirchlichen Theologie.*

[2] Winter, *Die neue Wendung in der Theologie.*

to the charge that his preaching led to "neglect and contempt of God's ordinances." [1]   That Wesley undervalued neither the Scriptures nor the means of grace plainly appears from his correspondence with William Law.   " In matters of religion I regard no writings but the inspired.   Tauler, Behmen, and a whole array of mystic writers are with me nothing to St. Paul.   In every point I appeal ' to the law and the testimony,' and follow no authority but this.   ' Seek,' say you, ' for help no other way, neither from man, nor books ; but solely leave yourself to God.'   But how can a man ' leave himself wholly to God ' in the total neglect of His ordinances ?   The old Bible way is to ' leave ourselves wholly to God ' in the constant use of the means He hath ordained." [2]

It is well, however, to learn from our critics and to ask ourselves whether we are as anxious to know " the mind of the Spirit " as to rejoice in His holy comfort ; whether we are as susceptible to His influences when He would place the seal of consecration on our bodies and on our spirits and so claim our whole life for God, as when He imparts the filial joy which is " the earnest of our inheritance " (Eph. i. 14).   In so far as Mysticism stands for a due recognition of the Holy Spirit's work in the heart of man, Methodism is rightly identified with it and claims to be a faithful exponent of spiritual religion as understood by the New Testament writers, and as illustrated in the experience of the saints of God.   But in other respects the critics referred to misunderstand Methodist teaching.   Wesley, in his sermon on " The Witness of our own Spirit," lays as much stress as any Ritschlian could wish on the Christian's " behaviour in the world " (2 Cor. i. 12, R.V.).   In this clear

[1] *Works*, vol. viii. p. 412.   [2] *Works*, vol. ix. pp. 406, 504.

exposition of the " ground of a Christian's joy" there is *no undervaluing of the objective factors of Christianity*, neither of the revelation in the written word, nor of the revelation in the Word incarnate. " No man is a partaker of Christ until he can clearly testify, ' The life which I now live, I live by faith in the Son of God '; in Him who is now revealed in my heart ; who ' loved me and gave Himself for me. ' " Nor does the religion described consist of pious feelings. The happy peace of the Christian does arise from the testimony of his conscience, but " in order to this there is absolutely required . . . an agreement of our hearts and lives, of our tempers and conversation, of our thoughts and words and works with the written word of God."

Modern attempts to identify Methodist doctrine with Mysticism are best understood in the light of *John Wesley's spiritual experience*. His indebtedness to the teachings of William Law and to conversations with the Moravians is as well known as his declaration that the mystical writings of Jakob Behmen were " sublime nonsense." The one fact explains the other : though under great obligations to Mysticism for spiritual light in which " everything appeared in a new view," Wesley was keenly sensitive to its perils and anxious to disavow its extravagances. Dr. Rigg has clearly shown that at a critical period in Wesley's religious life he was oscillating between Ritualism and Mysticism. As a doctrine of rest Mysticism was attractive to one who was vainly seeking rest in legalism. " This element represented the reaction, in such a true and earnest soul as Wesley's, of the inward against the merely outward." [1] But Wesley

[1] *The Living Wesley*, p. 90.

never passed from the extreme of servile legalism to the extreme represented by those mystics who disparage the outward means of grace. In a letter to his brother Samuel, he says: " I think the rock on which I had the nearest made shipwreck of the faith was the writings of the mystics ; under which term I comprehend all, and only those, who slight any of the means of grace." In the interests of spiritual religion Wesley often protested against the mere mechanical use of its most sacred ordinances ; but he called them " dead, empty forms " only when they were " void of spirit, of faith, of love," his supreme desire being to " shame nominal Christians out of that poor superstition they call Christianity," and to " convince them that such mean pageantry (for such it manifestly is, if there is nothing in the heart correspondent with the outward show) is absolutely unworthy, you need not say of God, but even of any man that is endued with common understanding." [1]

Mr. Abbey in his very able discussion of *Enthusiasm* bears witness that " neither Wesley nor the Wesleyans have ever yielded to a mischievous tendency which has beset most forms of mysticism. They have never, in comparison with the inward worship of the soul, spoken slightingly of " temples made with stones," or of any of the chief outward ordinances of religion. Their opponents often attempted to make it a charge against them, and thought, no doubt, they would be sure to prove it. But they never did so." [2]

Wesley believed as earnestly as any mystic in the testimony of the religious consciousness and in *the trustworthiness*

[1] *Works*, vol. x. p. 77.
[2] See *The English Church in the Eighteenth Century*, vol. i. ch. ix.

of the inward witness to the facts of individual experience. In his letter to Dr. Middleton, which Mr. Abbey justly describes as "one of the finest and most thoughtful passages in his writings," Wesley says : "If, then, it were possible (which I conceive it is not) to shake the traditional evidence of Christianity, still he that hath the internal evidence (and every true believer hath the witness or evidence in himself) would stand firm and unshaken." These words fairly represent the purport and spirit of the whole letter, and are a striking anticipation of Dr. Dale's argument in *The Living Christ and the Four Gospels.* Dr. Little in the Fernley Lecture for 1900 says truly that they have "an almost supernatural ring, so remarkable is their adaptation to . . . the Christianity of experience which has been the most notable development of modern Christendom."[1] But earlier in the same letter Wesley says, "I do not under- value traditional evidence. Let it have its place and due honour"; and there are other passages in his writings which fully bear out Mr. Abbey's statement that "taken by themselves [they] might seem to place Wesley among the ranks of those who *entirely distrusted* the evidence of inward feeling." But Wesley entirely distrusted neither the testimony of the Holy Spirit in the written word, nor His witness in the heart of man ; he never passed from the extreme of slavish adherence to the letter of Scripture to the extreme represented by those mystics who regarded the reading of the Bible as unnecessary on the ground that "it is only His letter with whom they converse face to face." Wesley attached supreme importance to "the marks and evidences of true faith which *the Scripture has*

[1] *Christianity and the Nineteenth Century*, p. 29.

promised," and powerfully urged that "these evidences must not be discarded as vain or delusive." But private revelations were not to be set "on the self-same foot" as the written word. "What I say now, I have said any time these thirty years, I have never varied therefrom for an hour : everything disputable is to be brought to the only certain test—'the law and the testimony.'"[1]

In his Journal, Mr. Wesley complains that "a spirit of enthusiasm was breaking in upon many, who charge their own imaginations on the will of God, and that not written, but impressed on their hearts. If these impressions be received as the rule of action, instead of the written word, I know nothing so wicked or absurd but we may fall into, and that without remedy."[2] The appeal to the Christian consciousness to confirm by its testimony the trustworthiness of the revelation contained in the divine word is quite legitimate in regard to all those truths which belong to the sphere of spiritual religion, for only in this way is it possible to vindicate the high claim of the Scriptures to be able to make men wise unto salvation.[3] But it is equally necessary to test all individual claims to spiritual revelation by the experience of the saints and by the written word. For such testing our Church has always made ample provision, as will appear when we consider Methodist doctrine and practice in regard to Christians' fellowship one with another and with God.

[1] *Works,* vol. x. p. 311 ; vol. ix. p. 143.
[2] Fourth Journal, *Works,* vol. i. p. 318.
[3] Dr. Armitage Robinson quotes a striking saying of Origen's : "He who reads will from his very reading experience a trace and vestige of inspiration in himself, and this personal experience will convince him that those are no mere human compilations which we believe to be the words of God."

Chapter the Ninth

COMMUNION WITH GOD IN THE CHURCH

Our fellowship is with the Father, and with His Son Jesus Christ.—1 JOHN i. 3.

> Still holy lives
> Reveal the Christ of whom the letter told,
> And the new Gospel verifies the old.—WHITTIER.

WHEN spiritual truth is expressed by means of natural metaphors, a strain is often put upon language, and the force of the illustration depends upon our perceiving the exact point at which violence is done to the ordinary meaning of words. Hence when St. Peter describes a Christian Church as " a spiritual house " and its members as " *living stones drawing nigh unto . . . a living stone* " (1 Pet. ii. 4, 5, R.V.), the very incongruity of the picture presented by the words when taken literally brings out with striking emphasis the thought that the Church is built up by the perpetual drawing nigh unto Christ of its individual members. These words of the apostle to whom the Lord Jesus said, " Thou art Peter, and upon this rock I will build My Church " (Matt. xvi. 18), help us to define the conditions of admission into Church fellowship and of continuance therein.[1]   As

---

[1] Note the recurrence in the *Rules of the Society of the People called Methodists* (§§ 4, 5, 6) of the words, " It is expected of all who desire to continue in these Societies, that they should *continue to evidence* their desire of salvation."

the " drawing nigh " of which St. Peter speaks is a continual
act and not an act done once for all, so the Church consists
of men and women *who are now coming unto Christ*, whether
they did once come to Him in the past or not.   The essential
condition is that each member of the Church should have
and should continue to cherish desires for spiritual life ;
for when such desires are not restrained but yielded to,
they incite to sustained efforts to attain their object.
This truth is forcefully expressed in St. Peter's words, for,
as Dr. Hort shows in his lucid exposition of the passage,
" the union of the many living stones with the one living
stone is not a quiescent juxtaposition effected once for
all.   It implies a perpetual conscious drawing nigh of
the many stones to the one stone, made possible and
made necessary by the fact that they live and that He
lives." [1]

Spiritual life comes *from contact with Christ and not
from incorporation into the Church*.   On this subject the
facts of history and experience confirm the teaching of
Scripture.   The upbuilding of the Church depends on the
intimacy of its members' communion with Christ ; therefore, the supreme purpose of its manifold ministries and
worship, the end of its fellowship and sacraments, must
ever be to promote spiritual religion, or, in other words,
to provide opportunities for that " personal approach of
the company of the living stones " which is " the instru-
mentality by which they are built up into a spiritual house."
It is by the indwelling of the Spirit of Christ in the hearts
of individual believers that the Church becomes a spiritual

[1] Commentary *in loco*, p. 105 ff.

house, wherein are offered up " spiritual sacrifices, acceptable to God through Jesus Christ."

Dr. Hort's utterances on this subject have a special value, and every word in the following statement deserves to be carefully weighed : " The new dispensation of the Spirit introduces or gives effect to a new conception of the manner of God's dwelling among men, not as in a material building among the other buildings of men, but *in the inner self of each, and so in the whole society* as united in heart and mind in His service (cp. 1 Pet. iv. 17 ; Heb. iii. 6). God dwells no longer in a house made with hands, as He once did, or rather once seemed to do, but in a society of men, whose acts as true members of the society are priestly acts on behalf of each other towards God." Against such a carefully balanced expression of the relation of individual believers to God and to each other, it is impossible to object that it renders Church and sacraments unnecessary. On the other hand, it affords no support to ecclesiastical theories which, as commonly understood, tend to obscure the fact that association with the Church and partaking of the Lord's Supper are not necessary guarantees of that direct personal contact with Christ which is the essence of spiritual religion.

Canon Gore praises Ritschl because " he perceived that it was through membership in the Christian common-wealth that men were to find their salvation." [1] On this, as on some other subjects, Anglican teaching manifests remarkable affinities with the school of Ritschl ; for if, in the one case, the individual becomes merged in the king-dom, in the other the Church rather than the individual is the immediate recipient of grace. Hence criticism directed

[1] See *The Pilot*, March 3, 1900.

against one theory applies for the most part to the other. Ritschl's position is clearly stated in these words : " The individual can experience the peculiar effect which proceeds from Christ only in connexion with the community founded by Him and on the presupposition of its existence. . . . The individual believer, therefore, can rightly understand his position relatively to God, only as meaning that he is reconciled by God through Christ in the community founded by Christ." [1]   Our inability to accept the teaching that we are the children of God because we belong to the " community of reconciliation " arises from no disposition to depreciate the great services which in the vast majority of cases the Church renders to the individual ; it is true that believers do find the Church in existence, and that most—we cannot say all—Christians " have been brought up in the Church, have in it become believers, and in it have been furnished with the right knowledge of Christ." But the Church is the " community of reconciliation " because its individual members rejoice in God through our Lord Jesus Christ, and strive by their testimony to bring others to share their consciousness that through Him they have now received the reconciliation (Rom. v. 11, R.V.).   Therefore, all who are " being saved " (Acts ii. 47, R.V.) are welcome to those sacred ordinances, which none can neglect without spiritual loss, though they become means of grace—real channels of blessing—only to those who in using them draw nigh to God.   All this, however, does not imply that Christian assurance, by which is meant personal certainty of salvation, can ever be a mere inference from the fact of membership in the Church of Christ.

[1] *Justification and Reconciliation*, p. 578.

A sympathetic student of Ritschl's writings, who finds himself unable to accept the doctrine that Justification has reference in the first instance to the community as a whole, and to the individual only as a member of the community, admits that "Ritschl does not distinguish between the historical and the religious significance of the community. Its historical significance appears in that it can lead the individual to Christ by instruction and example. But it must also point the individual *away from itself to Christ*, for in the deepest religious acts all historical mediation vanishes and the individual soul has to do with God alone. The importance of the doctrine of Justification is independent of the theory that the Church is the storehouse of the divine treasures of grace ; its central truth is individual assurance of salvation. Therefore, the doctrine of Justification does not require the subordination of the individual to the society." [1]

The interests of spiritual religion are endangered whenever the Church is so spoken of as to seem to *interpose between the soul and Christ*. Protestants have never denied that the fellowship and ministries of the Church are media — though not the exclusive media — through which the saving grace of God is conveyed to believing hearts. But as they read the Scriptures they find no warrant for the teaching that "the sacrifice and priesthood of Christ reach and touch each soul through its membership in the body"; [2] and as they read history they find that large accessions of grace have come to the community through individuals who were hindered rather than helped to draw near to Christ

---

[1] Wendland, *Albrecht Ritschl und seine Schüler*, p. 125.
[2] Canon Scott Holland. See *Priesthood and Sacrifice*, p. 152.

by the Church, which is sometimes spoken of as " the organ of contact" with Him. At the present day all Churches have need to lay to heart one of the lessons of Church history to which the late Dr. Creighton called attention : "The mediæval Church failed because it undertook to do so much for men's souls that men felt they were losing the consciousness that their souls were after all their own." [1] To deepen this consciousness must always be the supreme end of every act of priesthood in the spiritual house.

But if the interests of spiritual religion are endangered, however unintentionally, by doctrines of the Church which emphasise the priestly prerogatives of a class of men set apart for the discharge of sacerdotal functions, there are perils not less to be deplored which are the result of reaction from such views manifesting itself in *the neglect of Church ordinances, and the undervaluing of the privileges of membership in the Christian community.* Because the Church cannot do everything for the soul that is drawing nigh to God, it does not follow that it can do nothing. When the doctrine of the universal priesthood of believers becomes in Evangelical Churches a ruling idea in Church life as well as an essential element in Church theory, the fellowship of the Church will be more helpful, its ordinances more attractive, and its privileges more highly prized. Christian unity will also be promoted when, as Canon Gore desires, Evangelicals " emphasise the priesthood of the whole body in its rich positive meaning "; but, on the other hand, there is at least equal need that Anglicans, who emphasise the setting apart of individuals to represent the priesthood

[1] Bishop of London's Charge. See *Times*, February 22, 1900.

of the Church, should state as plainly as does Canon Gore that "those to whom such delegation is not made obviously do not become thereby less priestly as members of the priestly body." [1]

If, then, the Christian man is a priest unto God, his freedom of access to the divine presence is not merely a prerogative to be jealously guarded, but a privilege to be continually exercised in the interests of the Christian community. The whole body suffers loss whenever any member fails to use the means of grace as opportunities for personal fellowship with God. The priesthood of the believer cannot be delegated to any other man, however exalted may be his position in the Church. It is needful sometimes to insist on the negative aspect of this truth, and to maintain that the ministers of the Church have no exclusive right to the title of priest. But those who hold that every Christian is a priest should be the first to realise that *a positive obligation* rests upon individual believers to obtain for themselves and for others in intercourse with God those blessings which under the old dispensation it was the purpose of the priest's intercession in the holy place to obtain for the people.

Every soul that in lonely fellowship with God has been enriched with spiritual gifts has a treasure to dispense to others, and is qualified to contribute his share to the edifying of the Church. The highest end of Christian communion is attained when it enables us *to find God in the souls of other people.* "Our fellowship" with those who can say "the eternal life was manifested unto us" is "fellow-

[1] *Priesthood and Sacrifice*, p. 37.

ship with the Father and with His Son Jesus Christ " (1 John
i. 2, 3).   In fellowship with our friends we gain knowledge
of ourselves ; and when our fellowship one with another is
also fellowship with God, we gain a more intimate knowledge of the divine mind and will.   In this hallowed fellowship we learn how firmly based are the foundations of our
faith, though our own experience is neither a limit to the
spiritual attainment of others, nor a standard by which
to judge of the relative value of revealed truths.   Our
fellow-Christians' progress in the spiritual life may be a
revelation of energies available for us, which we have
failed to make our own ; their growth in spiritual understanding may be a revelation of fair domains in the inheritance of truth which we have not gone up to possess.

The value of *the argument from Christian experience*
has often been called in question, and the appeal to Christian testimony has sometimes been curtly dismissed on the
ground that the witness of the Christian consciousness
yields no valid evidence to those who are strangers to it.
John Wesley, in the remarkable letter to which reference
has already been made,[1] meets this objection in a practical
spirit and in forceful words.   To those who say, " This internal
evidence of Christianity affects only those in whom the
promise is fulfilled ; it is no evidence to me," he replies :
" There is truth in this objection.   It does affect them chiefly,
but *it does not affect them only.*   It cannot, in the nature
of things, be so strong an evidence to others as it is to them.
And yet it may bring a degree of evidence, it may reflect
some light on you also. . . .   What reasonable assurance can

[1] See p. 139.

you have of things whereof you have not personal experience ? Suppose the question were, Can the blind be restored to sight ? This you have not yourself experienced. How, then, will you know that such a thing ever was ? Can there be an easier or surer way than to talk with one or some number of men who were blind, but are now restored to sight ? They cannot be deceived as to the fact in question ; the nature of the thing leaves no room for this. And if they are honest men (which you may learn from other circumstances), they will not deceive you. Now, transfer this to the case before us : and those who were blind, but now see,—those who were miserable, but now are happy,— will afford you also a very strong evidence of the truth of Christianity ; *as strong as can be in the nature of things, till you experience it in your own soul :* and this, though it be allowed they are but plain men, and, in general, of weak understanding ; nay, though some of them should be mistaken in other points and hold opinions which cannot be defended." [1]

The personal witness of believers is inextricably bound up with the *witness of the word.* The Scriptures record the experience of patriarchs, psalmists, and prophets, of the companions of Jesus, and of the disciples who were first called Christians. The sacred writings are the supreme authority in the spiritual sphere, because in their pages alone men find a full revelation of God's will. Historical criticism cannot destroy this authority, nor invalidate the witness to religious truth of writers whose authority rests upon their knowledge of God and understanding of His

[1] *Works,* vol. x. p. 79.

ways. The Scriptures produce their credentials in every age, as sinners verify in their own experience the witness of the Spirit in the word to the exceeding sinfulness of sin and the depravity of the human heart; and as believers verify in their own experience the witness of the Spirit in the word to the power of divine grace to forgive and to strengthen, to enlighten and to sanctify. Hence in the words of "good stewards of the manifold grace of God" men hear "as it were oracles of God" (1 Pet. iv. 11, R.V.); and "the word of message" uttered by human .lips is recognised as "the word of God, which also worketh in you that believe" (1 Thess. ii. 13, R.V.).

The appeal to the Christian consciousness does not, however, imply that individual experience is either a standard by which to test the genuineness of the experience of other saints of God, or that it can set limits to the authority of Scripture. Words of God, which have become "spirit and life" to our fellow-Christians, but which we have not yet verified in our own experience, are not on that account without authority for us. Other words of God spoken by Him who bore witness to what He had seen and heard, to which neither we nor our fellow-Christians can as yet set our seal and say "God is true" (John iii. 33), are not on that account without ·authority both for them and for us. None can doubt that the Church of God has to-day a fuller and clearer understanding of His will than in any previous age, and this growth in divine knowledge is proof that *neither the individual nor the collective experience of Christians in any era can fix limits to the authority of the Revelation* which makes known to us how great is the salvation which God hath appointed us to obtain through our Lord Jesus

Christ. The experience of Christians yet unborn will confirm the truth of Pastor John Robinson's words, " God has yet more light to break forth from His holy word."

In every department of life, authorities are valued because they know more than we know ourselves ; hence their word is believed and their judgment trusted. There is, of course, good reason for recognising their authority ; but when that recognition is based upon clear and well founded convictions, it is inconsistent to say that only within the limits of our experience does that authority hold good. When, however, the argument from experience takes the form of personal witness to the truth of God's promises, His testimonies become the rejoicing of the believer's heart :

> He knows his path was trod
> By saints of old who knew their way to God.[1]

Moreover, Christian testimony is most powerful to reveal the glory of God *to other hearts*, when its radiance is the result of the blending of the inner light and the light of revelation. " Blameless and harmless " lives are the luminaries of the world, but there are dark places of life into which the Christian would hesitate to carry the lamp of witness, were he not sure that he is " holding forth the word of life " (Phil. ii. 16).

In the inner circle of Church fellowship the vigour of each member's spiritual life promotes the health of the whole body of Christ. Christian testimony, when it is based on personal experience, helps others to find the way to God, and establishes the claim of Scripture to be the utterance of men who " spake from God, being moved by the Holy Spirit " (2 Pet. i. 21, R.V. marg.). Thus " the saint alone is the real

[1] Hartley Coleridge.

proof of Christianity"; for if the Scriptures are the word of
truth, there will always be living witnesses unto Christ in the
Church in which the Holy Spirit dwells. When the fellowship of saints is a real communion of souls, it furnishes the
best safeguard against the perils to which the solitary mystic
is exposed. Mr. Inge truly says that " if there is any accusa-
tion which may justly be brought against the higher order
of mystics (as opposed to representatives of aberrant types)
it is this : that they have sought and found God in their
own souls and in Nature, but not so often in the souls
of other men and women." [1] Of the greatness of the loss
thereby sustained in the spiritual life we sometimes catch
faint glimpses, when human love becomes the stepping-
stone to higher levels of experience, and we know of a truth
that

> Through such souls alone
> God stooping shows sufficient of His light
> For us i' the dark to rise by. [2]

The fifth unwritten Gospel to which Harnack appeals
should not be limited to " the testimony of the *first* Christian community." The new life reveals itself to-day in
thousands of believers as a life which cannot be fairly described otherwise than as " a life in the Spirit, and again
as a life in love." Of the Christianity of the twentieth
century it may therefore be as justly said as of the Christianity of the first century, " This is a simple matter of fact
which no historical criticism can in any way alter." [3]
To the testimony in which Harnack finds *a fifth gospel,*

[1] *Christian Mysticism,* p. 316.
[2] Robert Browning, "The Ring and the Book," *Pompilia.*
[3] *Christianity and History,* p. 57 f.

St. Paul refers when he speaks of the Corinthian Christians as "living epistles." These epistles were written in his
heart, for the experience of his converts was to the apostle
sufficient proof that "the Spirit of the living God" had
written the epistles of Christ; but these epistles were also
known and read of all men, inasmuch as the lives of his
converts afforded proof to others that his ministry was
"not of the letter, but of the spirit: for the letter killeth,
but the spirit giveth life" (2 Cor. iii. 2–6). To him who
neglects Church fellowship this fifth Gospel is almost a
sealed book; these living epistles are imperfectly understood, or perhaps quite misunderstood, because they are
hastily read. Yet it may be that the experience of others
would furnish the element of proof which would add to
faith knowledge, and impart to faith full assurance.

"It is certain," says Novalis, "that my belief gains infinitely the moment I can convince another of its truth."
The range of this fine saying may be extended: it is certain
that my belief gains infinitely the moment I discover that
others have been convinced of its truth. But faith rests
solely neither upon individual experience, nor upon the
testimony of the Christian community; in our fellowship one with another we discover that the Holy Spirit
has spoken to our fellow-Christians as He has spoken to
us *through the word of truth,* and that to them as well as
to us God has fulfilled His "precious and exceeding great
promises" (2 Pet. i. 4, R.V.). It may well be that our friends
in Christ have proved that He is "able to do exceeding
abundantly above all that we ask or think," but instead
of doubting the reality of their experience, and making

our attainments the measure of theirs, we meditate on
" the power that worketh in us"; and though we cannot
as yet verify in our own experience their witness, we accept
it as an authentic seal to the truth of God's promises, and
pray that we " may be strong to apprehend with all the
saints what is the breadth and length and height and depth,
and to know the love of Christ which passeth knowledge "
(Eph. iii. 18, 19, R.V.). The true criterion for the religious
life is that which Aristotle in his *Ethics* laid down for the
moral life ; in the one sphere as in the other the greatest
weight should be attached to the judgment not of any single
individual, but of *the best men*. When, therefore, personal
testimony is in accord with the experience of the saints and
with the promises of God, it cannot be said that to appeal
to the Christian consciousness is to make conceivability or
caprice the test of truth.

The fellowship of the Church is a *fellowship in work*
as well as in word ; in the spiritual house it is the duty
and privilege of a royal priesthood to offer up " spiritual
sacrifices acceptable to God through Jesus Christ" (1 Pet.
ii. 5, R.V.). If due weight be given to the emphatic word
" spiritual," it may be freely granted that members of the
Church of Christ, who claim the privilege of their priesthood,
have need to remember that in "priestly acts *on behalf of each
other* towards God " the highest use of that privilege consists.
" The only sacrifices for the offering of which the spiritual
house of God was constituted, and which God who is spirit
could receive with joy, were acts of self-surrender on the
part of the living spirits of men. " [1]   That the Church as

[1] Dr. Hort, Commentary *in loco*.

a priestly community is called to serve humanity in the spirit of self-surrender and self-sacrifice is a truth on which it will be needful to insist when we consider the Christian's fellowship with God in the world ; but it is of equal importance to remember that every priest unto God is called to make *on behalf of his brethren in Christ* the spiritual sacrifice which consists in the consecration of self to the service of others. Out of such " love of the brethren " the wider " love " of humanity is evolved (2 Pet. i. 7, R.V.).[1]

"For their sakes I consecrate Myself," the Lord Jesus said in His high-priestly prayer : He was interceding " not for the world," but for the men whom the Father had given Him,—the men who believed on Him and knew His Father,—and through whose consecration to the work of His kingdom the unbelieving and unknowing world was to come by believing on Him to the knowledge of His Father. Herein, as in all things, He is our pattern: " for their sakes" should, in the first instance, mean to the disciple as well as to his Master, for the sake of the Christian community. When the members of the Church of Christ so fully partake of the Spirit of Christ as to be consecrated to its service ; when Christians recognise that fellow-disciples have the first claim on kindly sympathy, self-denying service, and fervent prayers,—then communion with God in the Church will be more intimate and more hallowed, the communion of the saints will be esteemed a precious privilege, and the Church will become a Brotherhood of peace,—a royal Priesthood, whose highest dignity consists in lowly service of the King of Love, by gentle treatment of the erring, gracious welcoming of returning wanderers, and persevering search

---

[1] ἐπιχορηγήσατε . . . ἐν τῇ φιλαδελφίᾳ τὴν ἀγάπην.

for those who have gone astray. St. Paul is writing to members of a Christian Church of the duties which they owe one to another when he says, "Walk in love, even as Christ also loved you, and gave Himself up for us, an offering and a sacrifice to God for an odour of a sweet smell" (Eph. v. 2, R.V.). To give up self for others is a priestly act; when the spiritual house is filled with the fragrant odour of such spiritual sacrifices, no other proof is needed that the members of the Church have the mind of Christ, who "loved the Church, and gave Himself for it" (Eph. v. 25).

In the sacred ordinance of which Christians delight to speak as "*the communion*," believers have fellowship one with another because they have fellowship with Christ. If there be real communion, it is *a spiritual act*,—"spirit with spirit must join." When Lord Tennyson was about to leave Freshwater for the last time, he was urged to receive the Holy Communion with his family; he consented, but was careful to explain that he received it in the Protestant sense, and quoted his own words, put into the mouth of Cranmer: "No sacrifice, but a life-giving feast."[1] The expression is a happy one, and suggests those aspects of the Lord's Supper which current controversies make it needful for us to emphasise:

> It is but a communion, not a mass;
> No sacrifice, but a life-giving feast.

If it is a life-giving feast, it is *not a sacrifice*; and inasmuch as our Lord instituted this memorial of His death at the time of the Passover, it is reasonable to suppose that we

[1] Tennyson, *A Memoir*, vol. ii. p. 412.

shall learn more about the Christian feast from the ceremonial of the Passover than from the ritual of the Levitical sacrifices.

There was only one way of celebrating the Jewish Passover; presence had no efficacy without participation—to keep the Passover was to *eat the Passover*. Hence at the Lord's Table Christians meet neither to witness the offering of the Eucharist by the priest, nor to worship Christ present on His altar-throne, but to partake of the memorials of His passion and to " feed upon Him in their hearts by faith with thanksgiving." The practice of non-communicating attendance tends to divert the mind from the significance of the symbolic acts of eating and drinking. It is true that the Levitical sacrifices were eaten by the priests alone whilst the laity worshipped, but it is a begging of the question at issue to assume that because some of those sacrifices were types of the atonement, they are therefore types of the sacrament which commemorates the atonement.

Opinions differ as to whether any light has been cast upon the Lord's Supper by the study of ancient sacrificial systems. Robertson Smith maintains that " the one point which comes out clear and strong (from the examination of ancient sacrificial systems) is that the fundamental idea of ancient sacrifices is sacramental communion, and that all atoning rites are ultimately to be regarded as owing their efficacy to communication of divine life to the worshipper." [1] But the antiquity of an idea cannot be regarded as determining its relative importance amongst the many ideas which are suggested by the words of our Lord and

[1] *Religion of the Semites*, p. 418.

His apostles. Many rays of light converge upon the Cross, and no-single idea embodied in sacrificial ritual can be more than a partial help to the understanding of the infinite significance of Christ's death. That it was an expiatory offering is foreshadowed in the Old Testament types, and clearly taught in the New Testament ; Dr. Salmond therefore does well to urge that the idea of "communion or participation . . . in a common meal has a subordinate place in the Old Testament, and particularly in the Levitical systems." [1]

No recognition of the Lord's Supper as a sacrifice is involved in saying that the ordinance instituted by Christ as a memorial of His death is *a spiritual feast*, life-giving in the sense which He Himself expounds in the discourse spoken at an earlier Passover : "The bread which I will give is My flesh, for the life of the world. . . . He that eateth My flesh and drinketh My blood hath eternal life. . . . It is the spirit that quickeneth ; the flesh profiteth nothing " (John vi. 51, 54, 63, R.V.). Disciples who come to the Lord's Table to celebrate the Christian Passover fix their eyes of faith on the

> very Paschal Lamb,
> Whose blood for us was shed,

and reach out hands of faith to receive the living Bread ; but it is spiritual food that is offered, and it must be spiritually assimilated if it is to impart spiritual strength and nourishment.

When these considerations are borne in mind, a prominent place may be given to the idea of communion to which

[1] *Priesthood and Sacrifice*, p. 77.

unquestionably some ancient sacrificial systems bore witness. The Christian Passover is not only the festival of an accomplished redemption by means of a sacrifice offered once for all, but it is also a sacramental meal. *Divine life is communicated* to all who draw near in faith, for the table is graced by the real presence of the Master of the feast, who is the Feast itself. To quote the weighty words of Professor Jevons : " The sacramental meal, wherever it exists, testifies to man's desire for the closest communion with his God, and to his consciousness of the fact that it is upon such communion alone that right social relations with his fellow-man can be established. But before there can be a sacramental meal there must be a sacrifice. That is to say, the whole human race for thousands of years has been educated to the conception that it was only through a divine sacrifice that perfect communion with God was possible for man. . . . Of all the great religions of the world, it is the Christian religion alone which is so far heir of all the ages as to fulfil the dim, dumb expectation of mankind : in it alone the sacramental meal commemorates by ordinance of its founder the divine sacrifice which is the propitiation for the sins of all mankind." [1]

So far as the communicant is concerned, a formal use of this spiritual ordinance is the danger against which, whatever be his views of the sacrament, he has need to be continually on his guard. The eating and drinking are acts symbolic of appropriating faith without which the benefits of His passion will not be spiritually received. *The real presence of each disciple* is as essential as the Real Presence of his Lord, for " the mystery of an actual com-

[1] *Introduction to the History of Religion,* p. 14 f.

munion with Christ is the mystery of the Holy Communion."
The hour of Holy Communion may be an hour wasted
in reverie, or an hour spent in storing up energy which
shall supply motive power for many hours of loving toil
amongst men for His dear sake. Communion with God
in the world is the evidence of the reality of the Christian's
communion with God in the Church ; and none worthily
partakes of the communion of the body and blood of Christ,
unless contemplation and emotion stimulate the will to a
real act of consecration to Christ's service amongst men :

> Here is my heart ; Lord, fill it up,
> That I may offer it as the cup
> Of Thy Communion to my fellow-man.

Chapter the Tenth

COMMUNION WITH GOD IN THE WORLD

The kingdom of the world is become the kingdom of our Lord, and of His Christ: and He shall reign for ever and ever.—REV. xi. 15 (R.V.).

It is a grand world if it were only made over again; and nothing awakens a keener interest than to see this going on.—DR. CAIRNS.

COMMUNION with God *in the world* may be intimate and constant. When our Lord sent into the world His disciples who were "not of the world" (John xvii. 16), He did not send them away from His presence. That their environment in the world would be hostile none knew so well as He who had to the uttermost proved how bitterly the world hates goodness. But in the world He was not alone, for the Father was with Him; and He promises that His little children shall not be alone in the world; all that the Father had been to Him, He will be to them: they shall not be orphans (John xiii. 33, xiv. 18, R.V. margin). He will environ their spiritual life: "Ye shall know that ye are in Me. . . . In the world ye have tribulation . . . *in Me* ye may have peace" (John xiv. 20, xvi. 33, R.V.).

In Ritschl's writings, so long as he is expounding his theory of knowledge, an impassable chasm seems to separate religion from science, but when he is dealing with *moral actions* no distinction is recognised between the secular and the sacred. Both with regard to the possibility of communing with God in the fulfilment of life's common tasks, and with regard to the paramount necessity of making worldly affairs subservient to the life of the soul, his teaching is often robust and stimulating. "In the practical domain the doors of the kingdom of God are thrown so wide open that all who are engaged in the promotion of knowledge and culture may enter in."[1] Ritschl does indeed sometimes make the Christian's relation to the world so prominent as to overshadow his relation to God, and it becomes needful to recall the fact that the great obstacle to spiritual religion is not the world, but sin. Herrmann also sometimes writes as though "God's nearness in the relations of our life" were an experience reserved for those who have what he understands by a comprehension of the Christ of history. Yet this influential school of thinkers has done well to urge upon the consciences of Christians the Reformers' doctrine that "moral life in our ordinary calling is an essential part of Christian perfection . . . that the calling of a citizen is no hindrance but a positive necessity to Christian perfection."

It was Luther's firm grasp of the doctrine of *the universal priesthood of believers* that led him to oppose the Roman Catholic ideal of a cloistered perfection. "Who is helped," he asks, "by thy cowls, thine austere countenance, or thy hard couch? Who comes thereby to the knowledge of God or to comfort of conscience? Or who is provoked by these things into love for his neighbour?" Since every believer is a priest unto God, the layman as well as the cleric may find in the discharge of the duties of his calling opportunities

[1] Wendland, *Albrecht Ritschl und seine Schüler*, p. 32.

for the exercise of the functions of his spiritual priesthood. The life of contemplation is not necessarily holier than the life of action; in the market-place saints may serve God in the temple of the spirit, whilst in the sanctuary men may draw near to the altar and yet be far from the altar's God. But such truths are perverted into mischievous error, when they are so emphasised as to lend plausibility to the assumption that the capable discharge of the duties of the earthly calling is the whole duty of man. In modern life spiritual religion is seriously threatened by false inferences from the maxim which affirms that Work is Prayer. A skilled workman is not, *therefore*, a pattern of all virtues; he may be neither an unselfish nor a spiritually-minded man. *Laborare est orare* is true only of those who have learnt that *orare est laborare*. True prayer calls into active exercise all the powers of the spiritual nature, and if hours of toil are to be also hours of communion the energies of the spirit must not lie dormant. Neither manual nor mental toil can achieve spiritual results; hence it is impossible to substitute the labour of the hands or the activity of the mind for the effort of the spirit. The cause of failure in the spiritual life, as in trade and study, is too often mere idleness; it is not of our earthly business that St. Paul is thinking when he exhorts Christians to be " in diligence not slothful; fervent in spirit; serving the Lord " (Rom. xii. 11, R.V.); St. Peter also puts us in remembrance of the fact that though we have promises of supernatural grace in order that we may " become partakers of the divine nature," the Christian virtues will never adorn our character unless *on our part* we add " all diligence " (2 Pet. i. 4, 5, R.V.).

It would promote clearness of thought and soundness of judgment, if the word "spiritual" were freed from suggestions of narrowness, which in popular discourse are often wrongly associated with it. Dr. Hort was of opinion that the *false implications of the word "spiritual"* are due to our habit of "assuming that the character of a feeling is determined by the nature of its object." In the interests of spiritual religion it is, therefore, needful to remember that, on the one hand, care for men's bodies may be as spiritual as care for their souls, and on the other hand, that a worldly spirit may be displayed in a church assembly as well as at a political meeting or a social entertainment. "Every fact in the world has a twofold aspect, the one material and temporal, the other spiritual and eternal. If the former appeals to us habitually and predominantly we are worldly, if the latter we are open to the access of faith. . . . A man is worldly or the reverse according to the interpretation which he instinctively puts upon the facts of his environment. . . . Heavenly-mindedness consists in interpreting the humblest fact according to the highest category, in seeking the spiritual content of each circumstance of everyday life. God presses close in common things,—the vision of the Presence alone gives free course to faith." [1]

The man who makes "his moral being his prime care" soon acquires a sensitiveness of conscience and a power of spiritual discernment which enable him to prove the things that differ and so to approve the things that are excellent (Phil. i. 10, margin). To such a man *the anti-spiritual is the worldly*; the charter of his Christian freedom

[1] Robbins, *An Essay toward Faith*, p. 74 ff.

includes "the world" amongst the "all things" which are his on the sole condition that he is Christ's (1 Cor. iii. 21–23). But if, in isolation from men and "exiled from eternal God," the soul surround herself with all things fair and say,

> All these are mine,
> And let the world have peace or wars,
> 'Tis one to me ;

then "the great house so royal rich" becomes "a crumbling tomb," and the soul desires "a cottage in the vale" wherein "to mourn and pray." In "The Palace of Art" Tennyson represents pleasures, not in themselves debasing, as yielding "no comfort" when they are sought for self alone. The palace was transformed into a prison not by the presence of evil things but by the absence of God ; therefore the soul is "plagued with sore despair, lest she should perish utterly," and the last verse of this noble poem contemplates the possibility of the soul's return to her "lordly pleasure-house," no longer "to sing her songs alone" :

> Perchance I may return *with others there*
> *When I have purged my guilt.*

On these conditions the doors of the world's treasure-houses are thrown open to the spiritually-minded. Painting, poetry, and music are never so worthily employed as in ministering to man's spiritual life, not necessarily by illustrating sacred themes, though always by suggesting true thoughts in regard to "whatsoever things are lovely" (Phil. iv. 8). A living painter has compared his work to the attempts of the child of an artist to do *something like* " the beautiful things he sees emanating from his father's studio," and he has reverently claimed for art a high place as the handmaid of religion : " No art or science, and indeed no possible acquirement, can really be desirable that does not do something to develop those qualities which distinguish humanity from the lower creation, the purely and consciously moral perceptions, and still more those qualities on the spiritually sensitive side." [1]

In the drudgery of life as well as amid the pleasures of life *a sense of the divine presence* is the one thing needful in order that earthly toil may become " a sacrifice divine," and that earthly joys may be a foretaste of heavenly bliss. " The *Practice* of the Presence of God " is the suggestive title of a booklet that has helped many to walk in the light of His face ; so eminent an authority as Professor James of Harvard has nothing but praise for the psychological insight which its teaching reveals. The words of Brother Lawrence, as recorded in these unpretentious conversations, show that although he had none of the learning of the schools he was taught of the Spirit. Hence he can accurately describe from his own experience, which many would call mystical, the conditions upon which the secret of the Lord is revealed to men : " In order to form a habit of conversing with God continually, and referring all we do to Him, we must at first apply to Him with some diligence : but after a little care we shall find His love inwardly excite us to it without any difficulty." To this holy man his duties in the kitchen were uncongenial, but he " accustomed himself to do everything there for the love of God " ;

[1] G. F. Watts, R.A., *Letter on the Relation of Art to Religion.* See the *Guardian*, October 3, 1900.

the result was that every day he had such fulness of joy in
the divine presence that, in his estimation, "the greatest
pleasures of the world were not to be compared with the
pleasures he had experienced in a spiritual state." This
Carmelite friar in the seventeenth century had a composure
of spirit to which many Christians to-day find it hard to
attain; and yet if spiritual religion be to us what it was
to him—the practice of the presence of God—we too may
preserve our heavenly-mindedness in the noise of the kitchen,
the bustle of commerce, or the mental absorption of the
study. "The time of business," said he, "does not with
me differ from the time of prayer; and in the noise of my'
kitchen I possess God in as great tranquillity as if I were
upon my knees at the Blessed Sacrament."

In fellowship with God the Christian learns the value
of his own soul and the capacities for blessedness of his
own spiritual nature, whilst in gaining such knowledge
of self he acquires the highest of all motives and the most
enduring of all impulses for *the service of humanity.* When
a man loves God with all his heart there is no room in his
heart for selfishness; to such a man the two commandments may be addressed: "Thou shalt love thyself"; and
"Thou shalt love thy neighbour" as thou lovest thyself
when God is thy supreme joy; for thy neighbour—prodigal
son or outcast daughter—may in fellowship with the Father
of Spirits come, like thyself, "to know and love God and
enjoy Him for ever."

With a true philosophic and religious instinct we call
societies for *doing good* "Benevolent" societies, *i.e.* associa-
tions of men and women who have *a good will.* Kant

proclaimed with characteristic vigour that " nothing can possibly be conceived, in the world or out of it, which can be called good without qualification, except a good will." Bishop Butler in his profound study of human nature showed that selfishness is not the only spring of human action,—that men and women can be benevolent if they will.   Mr. Kidd, it is true, has ably contended that religion is a supra-rational element in human nature, and that benevolent actions are contrary to reason ; but without accepting his theory that reason is essentially selfish, it is possible to recognise the important truth which is the basis of his argument, *viz.* that humane and benevolent impulses need *the support of religion.*   The good will does not act without motives ; philanthropists know that schemes for social improvement do not rest upon a secure basis, if they " assume that in the good time coming men and women will be willing to work hard and to love one another." But the essential principle of spiritual religion is that in fellowship with God the benevolent impulses of the heart may be strengthened by the Holy Spirit's energising ; it is, therefore, the bounden duty of Christians to prove the reality of their faith by facts,—to demonstrate to the world that communion with God does not mean withdrawal from mankind, but the gaining of power to work for God amongst men.

Practical mystics have always been the strength of the Church.   In the highest type of character deep insight into the things of God intensifies interest in all human affairs ; whilst zealous work clears the eyes of the soul for gazing upon the heavenly vision.   General Gordon possessed this " combination of religion and practical sense, of *mysticism and efficiency* "; this union of qualities often supposed to be opposites represents an ideal too seldom realised, but the reward of closer approximation to it is more complete equipment for the service of man. The mystic, whose danger is aloofness and lack of interest in the everyday concerns of ordinary people, may learn from the man of affairs how to focus his light on the real problems of life ; the practical worker, whose danger is the distraction which results from much serving (Luke x. 40, R.V. margin ; cp. 1 Cor. vii. 35), may learn from the contemplative disciple that the secret of calm devotion to the Lord's work must be learnt in meditation at His feet whilst listening to His word. Many Christians would do far more *work*, if they were mindful of a modern mystic's counsel: " Before giving, let us try to acquire. If you love yourself meanly, childishly, timidly, even so shall you love your neighbour. Before you exist for others it behoves you to exist for yourself. Let us beware lest we act as he did in the fable who stood watch in the lighthouse and gave to the poor in the cabins about him the oil of the mighty lanterns that served to illumine the sea. Every soul in its sphere has charge of a lighthouse for which there is more or less need. See that you give not away the oil of your lamp, though your lamp is never so small ; let your gift be flame, its crown." [1]

The gift of flame is a proof, which even the darkness can comprehend, that on the inward altar there burns brightly the sacred fire whose light is the pure flame of love. In the South of Europe the value of a plot of land

[1] Maeterlinck, *Wisdom and Destiny.*

is sometimes calculated by counting the number of olive-
trees that are growing upon it ; by a similar process it is
possible to estimate the value of a Christian Church ; its
power for good depends on the number of trees of the
Lord's own planting that grow within its borders, and
bear the fruit which yields light ; for " the fruit of the
light is in all goodness and righteousness and truth "
(Eph. v. 9, R.V.).

The Christian Church has not always proved worthy
of her name of honour ; this may be granted without admit-
ting that Christianity viewed merely as philanthropy is
a failure. It is an exaggeration to say that the lives of
Christians afford scanty proof that they share the anointing
by which their Master was set apart to toil and to suffer
for men. Moreover, the assumption that Christian conduct is specially blameworthy, unless it exemplifies a high
ideal of self-sacrifice, is powerful evidence that in the past
the disciples of Christ have not always misrepresented
their Lord and failed to manifest His spirit. All this and
much more might fairly be urged in reply to our critics ;
but it is wiser to learn from them, to acknowledge our
shortcomings, and to confess frankly that the Christian
community, claiming to be " a royal priesthood " ought
to bear more distinctly " the marks of the Lord Jesus."

The Church as a priestly community is called to serve
humanity in the spirit of self-surrender and self-sacrifice.
But in the " spiritual sacrifices " by which the Christian
priesthood serves the King *all forms of social service* are included. It is not enough to dwell on the negative implications of the word " spiritual," to insist that the sacrifices

are not material, and that the priests who offer them do not minister at earthly altars in temples made with hands. For whilst the term " spiritual sacrifices " cannot refer to ritual service, neither can it be restricted to acts of spiritual worship, nor to efforts to promote the spiritual welfare of men. " To do good and to communicate forget not : for with such sacrifices "—the sacrifices which consist in deeds of love and in sharing our blessings with others—" God is well pleased " (Heb. xiii. 16). Spiritual sacrifices involve always *the sacrifice of self*,—willing devotion to the work of Christ's kingdom ; but this devotion may be manifested in the various spheres of social service as well as in the more directly spiritual work of the Church. The Christian priesthood is royal, not because its members can boast of royal lineage, but because they are royal servants. They are slaves, for their Lord bought them and they belong to Him ; but they are also the servants of a King, and whilst in their spirits they offer Him the priestly service of intercession (cp. Rom. i. 9), in daily consecration to His work amongst men they present themselves unto Him whose love is their constraining motive, and by whose blood they were loosed from their sins and "made to be a kingdom, to be priests unto His God and Father" (Rev. i. 6, R.V.).

True notes are struck by those modern writers who maintain that Jesus aimed at a redeemed humanity, as well as by those who remind the Church that only by the faithful discharge of her priestly functions can she claim the kingdoms of the world for Christ and render to humanity the service which alone can prove her right to be called a spiritual house. " The House as the dwelling-place of God is defined simply by the presence of His indwelling Spirit, and these acts of self-oblation for the community are signs that His inspiring and uniting and ordering Spirit is indeed present." [1] Such "*acts of self-oblation for the community*" furnish the only evidence which will convince the world that the Spirit of Christ dwells in His Church; her upbuilding depends upon the constancy with which her members avail themselves of their privilege to perform holy acts of priesthood; and her power to bless the world will be in proportion to the efficacy of her prayers when she makes intercession for the transgressors, and in proportion to the completeness of her consecration when she offers herself to Him who came to seek and to save that which is lost. It is in communion with Christ in the world that His disciples are to continue His work, to share His sufferings, and to enter into His joy. "When I became a real Christian," says Lacordaire, "the world did not vanish before my eyes; it rather assumed nobler proportions; I began to see a noble sufferer, needing help; I could imagine nothing comparable to the happiness of ministering to it under the eye of God with the help of the Cross and the Gospel of Christ."

The demand which the world makes upon the Church to-day, and which it has a right to make, is but a modern version of the old demand: "Show me thy faith by thy works." The Church is asked to prove by sustained enthusiasm in the service of man that communion with God furnishes *a supernatural motive to benevolence*, a motive which will support and purify and strengthen every altruistic impulse in the heart of man. Redeemed men working for the

---

[1] Dr. Hort, *Commentary on 1 Peter* ii. 5.

redemption of humanity look at every aspect of the social problem in the light of the Cross ; therefore, their response to this demand should be twofold : on the one hand, a supreme concern for man's highest good ; and on the other hand, zealous co-operation with all who are striving to uplift mankind. At the Cross evangelistic ardour is kindled, for it is there that

> conscience wakes,
> And the heart in pain for its own red stain,
> For the *sins of others* breaks ;

but at the Cross the law of Christ is also learnt, there His yoke of service is placed upon the willing shoulders from which the burden of sin has rolled away ; henceforth " he that is weak " becomes to the loyal Christian " the brother for whom Christ died " (1 Cor. viii. 11), whose burdens it is a privilege to bear for Christ's sake and in the strength of His Spirit. It may be quite true that some schemes of social reform have no higher aim than the improvement of the environment of men, but if a man's surroundings are hindrances to his living " soberly and righteously and godly in this present world " (Tit. ii. 12, R.V.), such schemes will appeal more powerfully to the Christian because he is impelled to serve his fellow-men by a spiritual motive. From the Christian point of view improved sanitation, better dwellings, innocent recreations, and higher education are not only good in themselves, but they are also the possible means of enabling men to attain the highest good—to live in fellowship with God " the life which is life indeed " (1 Tim. vi. 19, R.V.). Hence the interests of " the life that now is " are increasingly regarded by the Church of Christ in her philanthropic activities, and in so far as they make for the godliness which it is her mission to promote, they have promise also of the life " which is to come " (1 Tim. iv. 8).

The social effects of Christianity are facts which furnish a firm foundation for faith ; they present a series of phenomena which no student of the history of Social Evolution can ignore, and the conclusions to which on scientific grounds such students have come furnish *an argument for the truth of the Christian religion* which appeals with great power to the modern mind. When the late Professor Romanes was the editor of *Nature*, he published an article by a missionary in the Sandwich Islands, who had occupied his spare time in making an exhaustive study of the land molluscs of the Archipelago. The writer of this article was introduced by the editor as " the most profound of living thinkers upon Darwinian topics," and his " generalisations reached after twenty years of thought" were described as constituting " a far-reaching argument both for Darwinism and for Theism ; for they rule chance out of the problem, and reveal a law whose source is invisible, but all-powerful, and which can be no other than the eternal, omnipotent fountain of all orderly movement." So high a value did Professor Romanes attach to the " analytical powers " of Dr. Gulick, the missionary referred to, that on Christmas Day, 1890, he wrote to this scientific correspondent for the express purpose of asking, " How is it that you have retained your Christian belief ? "

Dr. Gulick's reply holds an important place among the influences which led to Professor Romanes' return to the Christian faith, and inasmuch as the letter is not published in his biography its purport may here be given.[1] Dr. Gulick recognises that non-Christian systems of thought have " dimly apprehended that 'regard for the good of others' is the guiding principle of life"; he maintains that " the history of Social Evolution shows that in proportion as man gains faith in this principle and applies it intelligently, in that proportion has he advanced in happiness and dignity. . . . In populous regions there seems to have been a slow biological evolution through which altruistic instincts have gained increasing force ; but *no power outside of Christianity seems able to take man as he is, in any and every land, and set him on a new course.* The cause of this wonderful power in Christianity seems to lie in its ability to assure men of the Fatherhood of God as well as of the Brotherhood of man. Indeed, judging from my own experience and from what I have observed in China and Japan, it seems as if a strong hold on the latter idea, such as will awaken the enthusiasm of humanity, is attained only by those who are filled with the former. It should also be said that a strong sense of God's love does not remain with the man who refuses to love his neighbour."

In the socialising of Christian enterprise there is cause for rejoicing, but for *the spiritualising of all social movements* there is also a pressing need. It is not indifference to his brother's need, or narrow-mindedness, that prevents the Christian from resting content with reforms whose materialistic ideals might be fully realised, whilst men's characters remained unchanged. " I starve in soul, so may mankind," is an argument from experience, the force

[1] See *Bibliotheca Sacra*, January, 1896.

of which is so irresistible that when a man's soul-hunger
has been stilled he cannot leave his brother without the
offer of the Bread of Life. The Christian would not love
his neighbour *as he loves himself*, unless his chief concern
were that his neighbour should know the infinite joys of
his inheritance in the love of God.

Science finds the germs of altruism in the remote past,
for a purely egoistic life becomes impossible as soon as men
form themselves into communities, however rude their
organisation may be. Dr. Fiske concludes from his historical
survey of the evolution of humanity that " a society of
human souls living in conformity to a perfect moral law
is the end toward which, ever since the time when our
solar system was a patch of nebulous vapour, the cosmic
process has been aiming." Such a statement accords well
with the faith of the Christian Theist, who discerns behind
the cosmic process the good pleasure of Him who in many
ways fulfils Himself and has fully revealed His will in Christ :
it is the scientific way of describing " the eternal purpose
which He purposed in Christ Jesus " (Eph. iii. 11). But
everything depends upon *what is included in the cosmic
process.* " Social progress," according to Professor Huxley,
" means the checking of the cosmic process at every step
and the substitution for it of another which may be called
the ethical process. . . . Goodness or virtue involves a
course of conduct which, in all respects, is opposed to that
which leads to success in the cosmic struggle for existence."
And yet this clear thinker is driven to admit that the
ethical process cannot be excluded from the cosmic process,
for in a significant footnote, to which due weight has not
been given, Huxley states that " in rudimentary forms

of society love and fear come into play and enforce greater
or less renunciation and self-will.   To this extent the general
cosmic process begins to be checked by *a rudimentary
ethical process which is strictly speaking part of the former,*
just as the governor in a steam-engine is part of the mechanism of the engine." [1]

Christianity supplies a motive for doing good which is
effective in *combating the cosmic process* interpreted as meaning " the survival of the fittest," but effective also in *develop-
ing the rudimentary ethical process* which aims at fitting
others to survive.   Not only does it repudiate the " Gladia-
torial theory of existence " which applauds the successful
combatant who survives at the end of the ruthless struggle,
but it advances upon the teaching of natural altruism, and
for the maxim " Live and let live " substitutes the higher
but not contradictory principle " Live and help others to
live."   Christianity does not seek to harmonize by logical
methods the two commandments " Thou shalt love thyself "
and " Thou shalt love thy neighbour "; *solvitur amando,*
—the problem is solved by loving.   The nature of the man
who loves his neighbour as himself is not thereby impover-
ished but enriched.   Kaftan's noble saying is true : " The
good which is reduced by sharing is a lower good "; but
the Christian knows a good which is increased by sharing,
and for this reason he esteems it as the highest good.   The
experience of the man who loves God with all his heart
is that his spiritual nature expands ; and as his love for his
neighbour grows, he himself acquires more perfect knowledge
of " the love of God which passeth knowledge " and which
will for ever be " broader than the measures of man's mind."

[1] *Evolution and Ethics*, p. 57.

Evolutionists know that the fitness of a plant to survive depends upon its environment. On the bleak mountain height trees wither and die which are luxuriant and fruitful in the hot valley. In the new century the Churches that survive will be those that prove themselves most adapted to a social environment which will become more and more destructive of all parasitical growths of self-seeking or worldliness or pride. The Evangelical Churches must gird themselves for the task of proving that *the more spiritual the religion, the more social is its gospel.* "Do men gather grapes of thorns, or figs of thistles?" (Matt. vii. 16). When the thorny stock of humanity bears the fruit of kindness and goodness and love, men will recognise the result of spiritual grafting; nay rather, they will perceive that there has been a change of nature, which only the working of a supernatural force can explain. Professor Huxley says that "the theory of Evolution encourages no millennial anticipations"; but this pessimistic conclusion must be qualified by his own important statements in regard to the possibility of modifying the conditions of existence, and by his still more significant words: "Much may be done to change the nature of man himself. The intelligence which has converted the brother of the wolf into the faithful guardian of the flock ought to be able to do something towards curbing the instincts of savagery in civilised men." [1] Christianity does encourage millennial hopes, because it looks not to the evolution of intelligence alone or chiefly, but to *the evolution of love* which is faith's response to the knowledge of God. "The wolf shall dwell with the lamb, and the leopard shall lie down with the kid; and the calf

---

[1] *Evolution and Ethics.*

and the young lion and the fatling together ; and a little
child shall lead them. . . . They shall not hurt nor destroy
in all My holy mountain : for the earth shall be full of the
knowledge of the Lord, as the waters cover the sea " (Isa.
xi. 6, 9).

Thou that art born into this favoured age,
  So fertile in all enterprise of thought,
Bound in fresh mental conflicts to engage :
  Be not thy spirit contemplation-fraught,
Musing and mourning ! Thou must act and move,
  Must teach thy children more than thou wast taught, ·
· Brighten intelligence, disseminate love,
And, through the world around, make way to worlds above.
                  —LORD HOUGHTON.

PRINTED BY MORRISON AND GIBB LIMITED, EDINBURGH